SWEET TREATS

SWEET
TREATS

hamlyn

Published in the UK in 1998
by Hamlyn, a division of Octopus Publishing Group Ltd
2–4 Heron Quays, London E14 4JP

This edition published 2002 by Octopus Publishing Group Ltd

Copyright ©1998, 2002 Octopus Publishing Group Ltd

ISBN 0 600 60830 1

Printed in China

NOTES

Both metric and imperial measurements have been given in all
recipes. Use one set of measurements only and not a
mixture of both.

Standard level spoon measurements are used in all recipes.
1 tablespoon = one 15 ml spoon
1 teaspoon = one 5 ml spoon

Eggs should be medium unless otherwise stated. The Department
of Health advises that eggs should not be consumed raw. This
book contains dishes made with raw or lightly cooked eggs. It is
prudent for more vulnerable people such as pregnant and nursing
mothers, invalids, the elderly, babies and young children to avoid
uncooked or lightly cooked dishes made with eggs. Once
prepared, these dishes should be kept refrigerated and used
promptly.

Milk should be full fat unless otherwise stated.

Do not re-freeze a dish that has been frozen previously.

Measurements for canned food have been given as a standard
metric equivalent.

Nuts and nut derivatives
This book includes dishes made with nuts and nut derivatives. It
is advisable for customers with known allergic reactions to nuts
and nut derivatives and those who may be potentially vulnerable
to these allergies, such as pregnant and nursing mothers,
invalids, the elderly, babies and children, to avoid dishes made
with nuts and nut oils. It is also prudent to check the labels of
pre-prepared ingredients for the possible inclusion of nut
derivatives.

Ovens should be preheated to the specified temperature – if
using a fan-assisted oven, follow the manufacturer's
instructions for adjusting the time and the temperature.

Contents

Introduction   6

Chocolate   10

Favourite Desserts   36

Pâtisserie   50

Biscuits and Cakes   66

Sweet Gifts   80

Index   96

Introduction

If you are one of those people who have an ashamedly sweet tooth and who think that the first and main courses of a meal are nothing more than the prelude to the most important last course – the *pièce de résistance* – of a meal, then this is definitely the book for you. *Sweet Treats* will send you, blissfully and deliciously, into your seventh heaven!

This book contains a wide range of deliciously sweet dishes, including chocolate puddings, mousses and ice creams; richly luxurious delights, hot and cold, such as treacle sponge and creamy fruit fool; sweet pastries, the high point of the pastry chef's art, from apple tart to chocolate éclairs; scrumptious biscuits and cakes for tea and coffee-time treats; and, finally, a choice of mouthwatering gifts to shower on lucky friends and family members, such as nougat and chocolate fudge.

CHOOSING A DESSERT

There are many considerations you will have to think about when you select a dessert with which to end your meal. Are you cooking for a simple family meal, for example? Are you having an informal supper party for a few close friends or neighbours? Or are you throwing a formal dinner party to celebrate a special occasion?

Do you want to serve something delicious yet simple and easy to prepare, or are you looking for an impressive dessert that can be prepared at leisure in advance? The amount of time you have at your disposal is obviously a very important consideration.

Are you cooking for a large number of people, or will there be just a few of you? Is it summer or winter time, and will you be wanting to serve something cold or hot? What are you serving for the starter or main course? You don't want pastry, for example, to feature at every course.

These are all things that you will want to take into account. Remember that careful planning is the key to all successful cooking, so choose the dessert that will suit all your requirements.

USEFUL EQUIPMENT

You are unlikely to need any specialist equipment to make any of the dishes in this book, though there are certain items of equipment that are bound to come in useful, such as a food processor or an electric blender.

In addition to this, you'll obviously need a selection of good, sharp knives, including a small-bladed vegetable knife for paring and a large, steel chef's knife for cutting and slicing. Avoid knives that have carbon steel blades, which can easily be discoloured by the acid in fruit, transferring the discoloration back to the fruit. Remember to sharpen all your knives regularly, and store them carefully so that their blades do not become dulled by being continually clashed together.

A knife with a long serrated blade is the perfect choice for slicing delicate cakes and pastries. A swivel-bladed vegetable parer comes in handy for paring the rind from oranges and lemons. And a wire balloon whisk is useful for whisking egg whites and for whipping cream, since it helps to incorporate the maximum amount of air. A hand-held electric mixer can be used for both these jobs, as well as for mixing batters.

Other more specialist kitchen tools that can come in useful include an apple corer, a melon baller, a cherry pitter and a grapefruit knife, the curved serrated blade of which is the appropriate tool for hollowing out fruit and for removing stones and pips. A dipping fork, a long thin-pronged fork, makes coating confectionery easier although cocktail sticks can be used as a substitute.

A piping bag with a selection of differently shaped nozzles allows you to give an impressive professional touch to desserts and puddings with stylishly piped meringue mixtures and whipped cream decorations. A piping bag is essential, too, for piping choux pastry.

There are also certain dishes that are bound to come in useful, such as ramekins, pudding basins, and soufflé and charlotte dishes. Always try to use the particular sizes that are specified in the recipes, because they have been chosen deliberately to allow the pudding or dessert ingredients to produce exactly the right size and texture.

CHOCOLATE

The rich colour, unique texture and delicious flavour of chocolate combine to make it a favourite choice for a dessert or teatime treat. Plain dark chocolate is the most suitable for cooking; for the richest flavour and smoothest texture choose a brand with 70 per cent cocoa solids. Milk chocolate and white chocolate contain a lower proportion of cocoa solids and although their flavour is less intense than that of plain chocolate they make a good visual contrast. Chocolate-flavoured cake covering is an imitation chocolate and best avoided in chocolate cookery. Cocoa powder has a strong bitter flavour and is useful to accentuate the flavour of chocolate in cakes and puddings. Drinking chocolate powder, used to make hot milky drinks, is not the same thing and cannot be used as a substitute. For a guide to making chocolate decorations, see pages 24–25.

CHOOSING FRUIT

Fruit is undoubtedly one of the most useful ingredients in the dessert chef's repertoire. It is important, therefore, always to choose fruit that is at its very best to achieve the best results.

The ideal fruit is fresh, home-grown and sun-ripened. With modern lifestyles, this is not always within everyone's possibilities, however, and so it is important to know exactly what you are looking for when you are buying fruit in shops and supermarkets.

The finest fruit is not necessarily the biggest and brightest fruit in the shop. Fruit that is grown for its looks alone is not always the best tasting; try relying on smell to help guide you. If fruit smells sweet and fresh, it will probably taste that way too. On the whole, fruit that has skin, such as apples, pears, plums, kiwi fruit, pomegranates and mangoes, for example, should be firm – but not hard – with unshrivelled skins and without any signs of bruising.

Avoid fruit with brown patches, which may indicate that decay has started. This is particularly true of peaches and nectarines. Brown spots are perfectly acceptable on ripe bananas, but avoid ones with black patches, which indicate that the fruit is over-ripe.

Citrus fruit should feel heavy with juice and have firm, resilient skin with no blemishes or soft patches. Dessert melons should feel heavy and firm, without any soft spots or cracks. They should also have a strong scent. Soft berry fruits, such as strawberries and raspberries, should be of a uniform colour, with no signs of mould or rotting. Firm berry fruits, such as blueberries, should be plump and shiny. Cherries should also be plump, and should have firm shiny skins. Their stems should be green and not dry or dark-looking.

When you bring the fruit home, it should be checked over straight away. Packets of berry fruits, for example, should be picked over immediately, and any mouldy or soft fruits should be discarded before they have a chance to contaminate the rest of the packet.

Fruits that ripen slowly, such as oranges and apples, can be kept at room temperature, in a bowl, to ripen. Fruits that are already completely ripe should be kept in the refrigerator to prevent them ripening any further. Bananas are the one fruit that is an exception to this rule and should never be stored in the refrigerator.

BASIC RECIPES

There are certain dishes in this book which use basic recipes for things such as pâte sucrée (sweet pastry), crème pâtissière (confectioner's custard), and pâte brisée (rich shortcrust pastry). Recipes for these have been given in this chapter for easy reference.

ALMOND PRALINE
50 g/2 oz unblanched almonds
50 g/2 oz sugar

1 Place the almonds and sugar in a small saucepan and heat gently until the sugar browns and the almonds are beginning to split.
2 Turn on to an oiled baking sheet and leave to cool until brittle. Place in a heavy polythene bag and beat with a rolling pin until finely crushed. Praline can be stored in an airtight container for several weeks.

CREME PATISSIERE

300 ml/½ pint milk
1 vanilla pod
1 egg, plus 1 egg yolk
50 g/2 oz caster sugar, sifted
25 g/1 oz plain flour, sifted

1 Place the milk and the vanilla pod in a saucepan. Bring just to the boil, then remove from the heat and leave for 20–30 minutes.
2 Put the egg and egg yolk into a bowl with the sugar. Beat well until creamy, then add the flour and mix until smooth. Remove the vanilla pod from the milk, wash and dry it, and set aside for another recipe.
3 Reheat the milk until just below boiling, then pour it on to the egg mixture. Stir until blended, then return to the saucepan and place over a low heat. Bring gently to the boil, stirring continuously. If lumps form, beat well until smooth. Simmer gently for 2–3 minutes, stirring continuously. Leave to cool before using. Use on the same day.

Variation
If you do not have a vanilla pod, you can use 1–2 drops of vanilla essence, though this will not have quite such a good flavour.

PATE SUCREE
This is a crisp sweet pastry, ideal for flans and tartlets. It uses a higher proportion of butter than most of the other pastries that are used for these dishes. For best results, leave the butter at room temperature for several hours before using it. It should be soft but not oily.

150 g/5 oz plain flour
2 egg yolks
50 g/2 oz caster sugar
75 g/3 oz butter
1–2 drops vanilla essence (optional)

1 Sift the flour on to a board and make a well in the centre. Put the remaining ingredients in the well.

2 Mix the yolks with the sugar and butter, and gradually mix in the flour until the mixture has a crumbly appearance. Continue blending until a soft smooth ball of dough is formed.

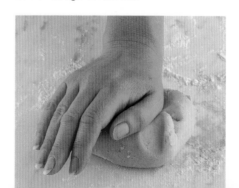

3 Because this pastry needs so much handling to incorporate the butter, wrap it in greaseproof paper and allow it to rest in the refrigerator for 20–30 minutes, until it becomes quite firm.

Using a food processor or blender
Pâte sucrée can also be made quickly in a food processor or blender. Put all the ingredients into the bowl. Switch on the machine until the ingredients are completely mixed, then knead by hand until the pastry is completely smooth. If the speed of your machine is variable, select a low one.

PATE BRISEE
Use this pastry for flans and tarts with a moist filling. It has a firmer texture than conventional shortcrust pastry and is therefore less likely to break. The traditional French way to make this pastry is directly on a board. Incorporate the sugar if you want a sweet pastry.

250 g/8 oz plain flour
75 g/3 oz butter, cut into small pieces
1 egg
pinch of salt
50 g/2 oz caster sugar (optional)
4–6 tablespoons water

1 Sift the flour into a bowl and rub in the butter with your fingertips until the mixture resembles fine breadcrumbs.
2 Add the egg, salt, sugar and sufficient water to mix to a soft dough. Knead lighly until smooth, being careful not to overhandle it or it is likely to become tough.

3 Put the pastry in greaseproof paper and chill in the refrigerator for 20–30 minutes before using.

Using a food processor or blender
Make in a food processor or blender as for pâte sucrée.

ROLLING OUT PASTRY
1 Knead the pastry as quickly and lightly as possible on a lightly floured surface. Take care to use as little extra flour as possible, as too much flour can upset the proportions of the pastry and can make it tough.
2 Roll out the pastry lightly and evenly, using short sharp strokes of the rolling pin. Turn the pastry as you work, bearing in mind the final shape you need, to avoid waste. Roll the pastry away from you, and turn it in one direction only.

BAKING BLIND
Flan and tart cases are often either partly or completely baked before the filling is added to ensure crisp results.

1 Once the flan case has been lined with pastry and the edges have been trimmed, prick all over the base with a fork. Then place a large circle of

greaseproof paper in the pastry case, with the sides of the paper extending above the sides of the pastry. Fill with baking beans or uncooked rice (the beans or rice can then be saved and used again at a later date for the same purpose).
2 Bake in a preheated oven for 10–15 minutes, or for the time indicated in the recipe. Carefully remove the paper and the beans or rice and return the flan case to the oven for another 5 minutes to cook through.

Variation
If you prefer, the greaseproof paper and beans can be replaced with a piece of crumpled foil.

Chocolate

Chocolate must be the most versatile of all sweet ingredients. It gives its irresistible flavour and unique texture to a great range of sweet dishes, from rich layered cakes to steamed puddings, from delicate mousses and darkly rich ice creams to tarts, pies and sauces. This chapter includes wonderfully delicious examples of all these, and other delights.

Chocolate Meringue Stacks

Preparation time: 40 minutes, plus cooling
Cooking time: about 2¼ hours
Oven temperature: 120°C (250°F), Gas Mark ½

- 2 egg whites
- 125 g/4 oz caster sugar
- 1 tablespoon cocoa
  powder, sifted

BITTER CHOCOLATE SAUCE:

- 175 g/6 oz plain chocolate,
  broken into pieces
- 150 ml/¼ pint water
- 1 teaspoon instant coffee
  powder
- 50 g/2 oz sugar

FILLING:

- 150 ml/5 fl oz double cream
- 2 tablespoons brandy
- 1 teaspoon clear honey

TO DECORATE:

- 8 piped chocolate shapes
  (see page 25)
- grated chocolate

1 Whisk the egg whites until stiff, then whisk in the sugar, 1 tablespoon at a time, until the mixture holds its shape. Carefully fold in the cocoa.

2 Line 2 baking sheets with baking parchment and carefully draw eight 7.5 cm/3 inch and eight 5 cm/2 inch circles on the paper.

3 Put the meringue into a piping bag fitted with a 1 cm/½ inch plain nozzle and pipe on to the circles to cover completely. Bake in a preheated oven, 120°C (250°F), Gas Mark ½, for *2 hours*. Transfer to a wire rack to cool.

4 To make the bitter chocolate sauce, place all the ingredients in a small pan and heat gently until the sugar has dissolved. Bring to the boil and simmer gently for *10 minutes*.

5 To make the filling, whip together the cream, brandy and honey until the mixture thickens and holds its shape, then spoon three-quarters of it on to the large meringue circles. Cover with the small circles.

6 Serve the meringue stacks on individual plates and decorate with the remaining cream and the piped shapes. Spoon some of the bitter chocolate sauce around each one and sprinkle with a little grated chocolate.

Makes 8

Pears à la Belle Hélène

Preparation time: 20 minutes, plus cooling
Cooking time: 25–35 minutes

- 900 ml/1½ pints water
- 175 g/6 oz sugar
- pared rind of 1 orange
- 6 pears
- 2 tablespoons chopped almonds, browned, to decorate

CHOCOLATE ORANGE SAUCE:
- 125 g/4 oz plain chocolate, broken into pieces
- juice of 1 orange
- 175 g/6 oz can evaporated milk
- 2 tablespoons Cointreau

1 Put the water, sugar and orange rind in a saucepan, and heat gently until the sugar has dissolved.

2 Peel the pears, leaving the stalks on, place in the syrup, cover and poach very gently over a low heat for *20–30 minutes*. Leave to cool in the syrup with the lid on.

3 Remove the pears with a slotted spoon. Halve, discarding the cores, and place on individual serving dishes.

4 To make the chocolate orange sauce, place all the ingredients, except the Cointreau, in a small pan and heat gently until melted. Bring to the boil and simmer for *3 minutes*, then add the Cointreau.

5 Spoon the chocolate orange sauce over the pears and sprinkle with the almonds.

Serves 6

Chocolate Liqueur Crêpes

Preparation time: 30 minutes, plus standing
Cooking time: 25–30 minutes
Oven temperature: 200°C (400°F), Gas Mark 6

- 125 g/4 oz plain flour
- 1 tablespoon cocoa powder
- 1 tablespoon soft brown sugar
- 1 egg, beaten
- 300 ml/½ pint milk
- 1 tablespoon oil, plus extra for frying
- shredded orange rind, to finish

FILLING:
- 2 tablespoons cornflour
- 2 tablespoons caster sugar
- 150 ml/¼ pint milk
- 2 eggs, separated

- 50 g/2 oz plain chocolate, finely chopped
- 2 tablespoons Grand Marnier
- grated rind of 1 orange

GLAZE:
- 25 g/1 oz butter, melted
- icing sugar, to sprinkle

CHOCOLATE ORANGE SAUCE:
- 125 g/4 oz plain chocolate, broken into pieces
- juice of 1 orange
- 175 g/6 oz can evaporated milk
- 2 tablespoons Cointreau

1 Sift the flour and cocoa into a bowl and make a well in the centre. Add the sugar and egg, then gradually add half the milk, stirring constantly until a thick batter is formed. Add the oil and beat thoroughly until smooth. Add the remaining milk and leave to stand for *30 minutes*.

2 Heat a 15 cm/6 inch omelette pan and add a few drops of oil. Pour in 1 tablespoon of the batter and tilt the pan to coat the bottom evenly. Cook until the underside is brown, then turn over and cook for another *10 seconds*. Turn out on to a wire rack. Repeat with the remaining batter, stacking the cooked crêpes one on top of the other.

3 To make the filling, blend the cornflour and sugar with a little of the milk. Bring the remaining milk to the boil and pour on to the blended cornflour, stirring. Return to the pan and cook for *3 minutes*, until thickened. Stir in the egg yolks. Add the chocolate, stirring until melted, then stir in the Grand Marnier and orange rind.

4 Whisk the egg whites until stiff then fold into the chocolate mixture.

5 Spoon 1 tablespoon of the mixture on to each crêpe and fold into quarters to make a triangular shape, enclosing the filling. Place on a greased baking sheet. Brush with the melted butter and sprinkle with icing sugar.

6 Bake in a preheated oven, 200°C (400°F), Gas Mark 6, for *10–15 minutes*.

7 To make the chocolate orange sauce, place all the ingredients, except the Cointreau, in a small pan and heat gently until melted. Bring to the boil and simmer for *3 minutes*, then add the Cointreau.

8 Place the crêpes on a warmed serving dish, pour over a little warm chocolate orange sauce and sprinkle with orange rind. Serve the remaining sauce separately.

Serves 6–8

White and Dark Truffle Cake

Preparation time: 45 minutes, plus cooling and chilling
Cooking time: 12–14 minutes
Oven temperature: 190°C (375°F), Gas Mark 5

- 2 eggs
- 50 g/2 oz caster sugar
- 3 tablespoons cornflour
- 2 tablespoons cocoa powder
- 2 tablespoons cold strong
  black coffee
- 1 tablespoon whisky

DARK LAYERS:
- 400 g/13 oz plain chocolate
- 475 ml/16 fl oz double cream

WHITE LAYER:
- 200 g/7 oz white chocolate
- 300 ml/½ pint double cream

TO DECORATE:
- frosted rose petals (see
  page 72)

1 Grease and line the base of a 23 cm/9 inch springform tin and grease again.

2 In a large bowl over barely simmering water, whisk the eggs with the sugar for *5–7 minutes* until thick and creamy. Remove from the heat.

3 Sift the cornflour and cocoa three times into a bowl. Fold into the egg mixture until no streaks remain. Turn into the prepared tin, spreading evenly.

4 Bake in a preheated oven, 190°C (375°F), Gas Mark 5, for about *7 minutes* until risen. Cool for *10 minutes* in the tin. Remove to a wire rack and leave to cool completely. Wash and thoroughly dry the tin; carefully return the cooled cake. Combine the coffee and whisky and evenly brush or drizzle over the cake.

5 To make the first dark layer, melt half the chocolate in a bowl over simmering water. Leave to cool. Beat half of the cream until thick; fold in the chocolate until smooth. Spread evenly over the cake in the tin. Bang the tin on a work surface once or twice to remove any air bubbles. Cover and place in the refrigerator.

6 To make the white layer, melt the white chocolate in a bowl over simmering water. Remove from the heat. Leave to cool. Beat the cream until thick. Fold in the cooled white chocolate until smooth. Spread evenly over the dark layer in the tin. Bang the tin on the work surface to remove any air bubbles. Cover and chill.

7 To make the second dark layer, prepare as directed in step 5, using the remaining dark layer ingredients. Pour over the white layer, bang the tin again, then smooth the surface. Cover and chill for *several hours* until set.

8 To serve, remove the sides of the tin. Place the cake on a serving plate and sprinkle with the frosted rose petals.

Serves 8–10

Double Chocolate Chip Ice Cream

Preparation time: 10 minutes, plus freezing
Cooking time: about 15 minutes

- 90 g/3½ oz plain chocolate, broken into pieces
- 300 ml/½ pint milk
- 3 egg yolks
- 75 g/3 oz sugar
- 300 ml/½ pint double or whipping cream, whipped to soft peaks
- 65 g/2½ oz plain chocolate, chopped
- wafer biscuits, to decorate

1 Stir the chocolate pieces with the milk in a saucepan over a low heat, until the chocolate melts and the mixture is smooth.

2 Whisk the egg yolks with the sugar in a mixing bowl, until the mixture falls off the whisk in a thick ribbon. Gradually add the chocolate-flavoured milk, whisking constantly. Pour the mixture back into the saucepan and stir over a medium heat, until it thickens and coats the back of the spoon.

3 Strain into a bowl and cool in the refrigerator or stir over a bowl of ice. When cold, fold in the whipped cream.

4 If using an ice cream maker, pour the mixture into it, add the chopped chocolate and follow the manufacturer's instructions.

5 If using a freezer, pour the mixture into a freezer container and freeze until the ice cream begins to set around the edges. Pour into a mixing bowl, add the chopped chocolate and whisk until the ice cream is smooth. Return to the freezer container and freeze for *30 minutes*. Repeat whisking and freezing at *30-minute* intervals until the ice cream thickens, then leave until set. Serve the ice cream decorated with wafer biscuits.

Serves 6–8

Profiteroles

Preparation time: 30 minutes, plus cooling
Cooking time: 40–45 minutes
Oven temperature: 220°C (425°F), Gas Mark 7

CHOUX PASTRY:

- 50 g/2 oz butter or margarine
- 150 ml/¼ pint water
- 65 g/2½ oz plain flour, sifted
- 2 eggs, beaten

FILLING:

- 175 ml/6 fl oz double cream,
  whipped

BITTER CHOCOLATE SAUCE:

- 175 g/6 oz plain chocolate,
  broken into pieces
- 150 ml/¼ pint water
- 1 teaspoon instant coffee
  powder
- 50 g/2 oz sugar

1 Melt the butter or margarine in a large pan, add the water and bring to the boil. Add the flour all at once and beat thoroughly until the mixture leaves the side of the pan. Cool slightly, then beat in the eggs vigorously, a little at a time. Put the mixture into a piping bag fitted with a plain 1 cm/½ inch nozzle and pipe small mounds on a dampened baking sheet.

2 Bake in a preheated oven, 220°C (425°F), Gas Mark 7, for *10 minutes*, then lower the heat to 190°C (375°F), Gas Mark 5, and bake for a further *20–25 minutes*, until golden brown. Make a slit in the side of each profiterole and place on a wire rack to cool.

3 Put the cream in a piping bag fitted with a 3 mm/⅛ inch plain nozzle and pipe a little into each profiterole.

4 To make the bitter chocolate sauce, place all the ingredients in a small pan and heat gently until the sugar has dissolved. Bring to the boil and simmer gently for *10 minutes*.

5 Pile the profiteroles into a pyramid on a serving dish and pour over the chocolate sauce just before serving.

Serves 4–6

Chocolate Roulade

Preparation time: 30 minutes, plus cooling and chilling
Cooking time: 25–30 minutes
Oven temperature: 180°C (350°F), Gas Mark 4

- 150 g/5 oz plain chocolate,
  broken into pieces
- 3 tablespoons water
- 4 eggs, separated
- 150 g/5 oz caster sugar

TO FINISH:

- 300 ml/½ pint double cream,
  whipped
- sifted icing sugar
- chocolate rose leaves
  (see page 25)

1 Place the chocolate and water in a saucepan and heat gently until melted.

2 Whisk the egg yolks in a large bowl with half the sugar until thick and creamy, then whisk in the warm chocolate.

3 Whisk the egg whites until stiff, then whisk in the remaining sugar. Fold into the chocolate mixture.

4 Turn into a lined and greased 20 x 30 cm/8 x 12 inch Swiss roll tin and bake in a preheated oven, 180°C (350°F), Gas Mark 4, for *25–30 minutes*, until firm.

5 Leave the roulade to cool for *5 minutes*, then cover with a clean damp cloth and leave in the refrigerator overnight.

6 The next day, carefully remove the cloth and turn the roulade on to a sheet of greaseproof paper sprinkled thickly with icing sugar. Peel off the lining paper.

7 Spread three-quarters of the cream evenly over the roulade and roll up like a Swiss roll. Transfer to a serving dish, pipe the remaining cream on the top and decorate with chocolate rose leaves.

Serves 8

Devil's Food Cake

Preparation time: 35 minutes, plus cooling
Cooking time: 45–50 minutes
Oven temperature: 190°C (375°F), Gas Mark 5

- 75 g/3 oz plain chocolate, broken into pieces
- 175 ml/6 fl oz strong black coffee
- 175 g/6 oz unsalted butter
- 250 g/8 oz soft dark brown sugar
- 50 g/2 oz vanilla sugar
- 3 eggs
- 300 g/10 oz plain flour
- 1½ teaspoons bicarbonate of soda
- 175 ml/6 fl oz soured cream

ICING:

- 500 g/1 lb sugar
- 300 ml/½ pint water
- 2 egg whites, stiffly beaten

1 Grease three 20 cm/8 inch sandwich tins and line with greaseproof paper. Brush the paper with melted butter and dust with flour.

2 Place the chocolate in a saucepan with the coffee, stir over a low heat until the chocolate melts and the mixture is smooth. Leave to cool.

3 Beat the butter in a mixing bowl until pale and soft. Add the sugars and beat until fluffy. Add the eggs, 1 at a time, beating well after each addition. Stir in the chocolate mixture. Sift the flour and bicarbonate of soda together on to a sheet of greaseproof paper and gently fold in one-third of the flour then one-third of the soured cream. Repeat until all the flour and soured cream are incorporated.

4 Divide the mixture between the prepared tins and bake in a preheated oven, 190°C (375°F), Gas Mark 5, for *25 minutes* or until a skewer inserted into the centre comes out clean. Remove from the oven and leave in the tins on a wire rack for *5 minutes* before turning out to cool completely.

5 To make the icing, place the sugar and water in a heavy-based saucepan and stir over a medium heat until the sugar dissolves. Brush away any sugar crystals that have formed on the sides of the pan with a pastry brush dipped in cold water. Increase the heat and bring to the boil. Simmer until the mixture reaches the soft ball stage. Test by putting a little of the mixture into a glass of iced water. It should form soft, sticky balls. Remove from the heat and dip the base of the pan in cold water to arrest further cooking.

6 Gradually whisk the syrup into the beaten egg whites. Continue beating until the icing thickens and loses its sheen. Spread immediately between the cake layers and over the top and sides.

Makes one 3-layer 20 cm/8 inch cake

Chocolate decorations

Chocolate rates high among many people's favourite foods. Plain chocolate gives the best results for making decorations. Choose a chocolate that contains a high proportion of cocoa solids – around 70 per cent is best. Break it into small squares and place in a bowl over a pan of hot water. Heat gently until the chocolate melts.

Chocolate caraque

Grated chocolate

Chocolate shapes

Chocolate-dipped almonds, hazelnuts and Brazil nuts

Chocolate caraque is made by spreading a thin layer of melted chocolate on a clean work surface. Leave until just firm but not quite hard. Using a sharp knife at an angle, scrape off a thin layer of chocolate with a slight sawing motion.

Chocolate-dipped almonds, hazelnuts and Brazil nuts are made by spearing the nuts with a fine skewer and dipping them into melted chocolate, to cover completely or partially. Tap the skewer against the dish to drain off excess chocolate, then place on nonstick baking paper to dry.

Grated chocolate is made using a hand-held cheese grater, the grating disc of a food processor, or a rotary hand grater. Chill a block of chocolate for 20 minutes and grate straight from the block.

Chocolate shapes are made by spreading a thin layer of melted chocolate on a piece of foil or greaseproof paper. Leave until set, then cut into shapes using a sharp knife.

Chocolate shavings are made with a potato peeler. Chill the chocolate first.

Piped chocolate shapes should be piped onto nonstick baking paper. Fill a greaseproof paper piping bag with melted chocolate. Cool slightly, snip off the end and pipe designs. Leave to set, then peel off the paper.

Chocolate-dipped strawberries are made in the same way as nuts.

Chocolate-dipped physalis also work well, as do grapes, orange segments and pieces of pineapple.

Chocolate rose leaves are made using fresh leaves with clearly marked veins. Wash and dry them, then coat the undersides with melted chocolate using a fine paintbrush. Allow to set, chocolate side up, then gently peel the rose leaf away from the chocolate.

Chocolate shavings

Chocolate-dipped strawberries

Chocolate-dipped physalis

Chocolate rose leaves

Piped chocolate shapes

Chocolate Mousse

Preparation time: 10 minutes, plus chilling
Cooking time: 2–3 minutes

- 4 eggs, separated
- 125 g/4 oz caster sugar
- 125 g/4 oz plain chocolate, broken into pieces
- 3 tablespoons water
- 300 ml/½ pint double cream

TO DECORATE:

- 65 ml/2½ fl oz whipping cream, whipped to firm peaks
- chocolate shavings (see page 25)

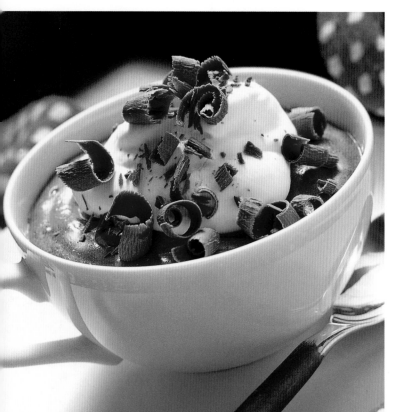

1 Put the egg yolks and sugar into a bowl and whisk with an electric beater until thick and mousse-like.

2 Melt the chocolate with the water in a heatproof bowl set over a pan of simmering water. Remove from the heat and let cool slightly, then whisk into the egg mixture.

3 Whip the cream until it stands in soft peaks, then carefully fold into the chocolate mixture.

4 Whisk the egg whites until stiff, carefully fold 1 tablespoon into the mousse, and then fold in the rest. Pour into 4–6 cups or small dishes and chill until set.

5 To serve, top each mousse with whipped cream, then sprinkle over the chocolate shavings.

Serves 4–6

variation

Chocolate Orange Mousse

Follow step 1 of the main recipe; then whisk into the mousse-like mixture the finely grated rind of 1 orange and 1 tablespoon of Cointreau. Proceed as for the main recipe.

Chocolate Fondue

Preparation time: 5 minutes
Cooking time: about 5 minutes

- 90 g/3½ oz Swiss Mountain
  or Toblerone chocolate
- 50 g/2 oz plain chocolate
- 2 tablespoons double cream
- 1 tablespoon rum

TO SERVE:

- selection of fruit including
  strawberries, raspberries,
  cherries, sliced banana
- sponge fingers or *langues de
  chats*

1 Break the Swiss Mountain or Toblerone chocolate and plain chocolate into a heatproof bowl and add the cream. Place over a saucepan of gently simmering water. Stir until the chocolate has melted. Stir in the rum and continue to heat, stirring, for *1 minute*.

2 Pour the sauce into a warmed heatproof bowl. Serve with a selection of fruits and biscuits for dipping, using bamboo skewers to spear the fruit.

Serves 4

Steamed Chocolate Sponge

Preparation time: 30 minutes
Cooking time: about 1½ hours

- 125 g/4 oz butter
- 125 g/4 oz caster sugar
- 2 eggs, beaten
- 150 g/5 oz self-raising flour, sifted
- 20 g/¾ oz cocoa powder mixed with 2 tablespoons milk

CHOCOLATE SAUCE:

- 25 g/1 oz unsalted butter
- 125 g/4 oz plain chocolate, broken into squares
- 25 ml/1 fl oz double cream

1 Grease a 900 ml/1½ pint pudding basin.

2 Cream the butter and sugar together in a bowl until light and fluffy. Gradually add the eggs, beating well between each addition. Fold in the flour until thoroughly blended, using a figure-of-eight motion. Add the cocoa and milk mixture.

3 Spoon the sponge mixture into the prepared pudding basin. Cover with a pleated piece of greased greaseproof paper and a sheet of foil large enough to allow for expansion and tie with string.

4 Place the basin in a large heavy-based saucepan, two-thirds full of hot water. Cover and steam over a low heat for about *1½ hours*, topping up with more hot water as and when necessary.

5 While the pudding is steaming, prepare the chocolate sauce. Put the butter and chocolate into a heatproof bowl set over a pan of simmering water. When the chocolate has melted, beat in the double cream. If the sauce is not being served immediately, keep it warm over a very low heat.

6 To serve, remove the string, paper and foil and turn out the pudding on to a warmed serving dish. Pour a little hot chocolate sauce over the pudding and serve the rest separately.

Serves 4–6

variation
Mocha Sauce

Instead of the chocolate sauce, make a mocha sauce to serve with the steamed pudding. Melt 25 g/1 oz butter over a low heat, add 25 g/1 oz plain flour and cook for *2 minutes*, stirring. Add 600 ml/1 pint milk and bring to the boil. Reduce the heat, add 50 g/2 oz caster sugar and 1 tablespoon each of cocoa powder and instant coffee powder and cook until dissolved. Serve the sauce hot.

Double Chocolate Brownies

Preparation time: 20 minutes, plus cooling
Cooking time: 35 minutes
Oven temperature: 190°C (375°F), Gas Mark 5

- 375 g/12 oz white chocolate
- 50 g/2 oz unsalted butter
- 250 g/8 oz plain chocolate
- 3 eggs
- 150 g/5 oz caster sugar
- 175 g/6 oz self-raising flour
- 1 teaspoon almond essence
- 150 g/5 oz broken walnuts

1 Grease and line a 28 cm x 20 cm/11 x 8 inch shallow baking tin with greaseproof paper.

2 Break up 125 g/4 oz of the white chocolate and put it into a heatproof bowl with the butter. Leave over a saucepan of simmering water until melted. Stir lightly.

3 Roughly chop the remaining white and plain chocolate.

4 Whisk together the eggs and sugar in a large bowl until foamy. Beat in the melted chocolate mixture. Sift the flour into the bowl and stir it into the mixture with the almond essence, walnuts and chopped white and plain chocolate.

5 Turn the brownie mixture into the prepared tin and bake in a preheated oven, 190°C (375°F), Gas Mark 5, for *35 minutes* until risen and just firm. Leave the baked mixture in the tin on a wire rack to cool.

6 When cool, turn out of the tin on to a board and cut into the traditional brownie squares or rectangles.

Makes 14–16

Bananas with Chocolate Fudge Sauce

Preparation time: 10 minutes
Cooking time: 20 minutes
Oven temperature: 180°C (350°F), Gas Mark 4

- 4 firm bananas, skins left on
- 1 tablespoon lemon juice
- lightly whipped cream or
  vanilla ice cream, to serve
- chocolate shavings, to
  decorate

SAUCE:

- 100 ml/3½ fl oz double cream
- 125 g/4 oz plain chocolate,
  broken into pieces
- 25 g/1 oz unsalted butter
- 125 g/4 oz golden syrup

1 Place the bananas in a shallow ovenproof dish. Brush the skins with the lemon juice and bake in a preheated oven, 180°C (350°F), Gas Mark 4, for *20 minutes* or until the bananas have darkened in colour and feel soft.

2 Meanwhile, make the sauce. Put the cream, chocolate, butter and golden syrup in a small, heavy-based saucepan. Heat gently, stirring frequently, until the chocolate has melted. Bring to the boil and boil for *2 minutes* until thickened slightly.

3 Transfer the bananas to warmed serving plates. Split lengthways to reveal the flesh. Top with cream or ice cream, decorate with chocolate shavings and serve with the hot fudge sauce.

Serves 4

Chocolate Fudge Cake

Preparation time: 45 minutes, plus cooling
Cooking time: 1¼–1½ hours
Oven temperature: 160°C (325°F) Gas Mark 3

CAKE:
- **250 ml/8 fl oz milk**
- **1 tablespoon lemon juice**
- **125 g/4 oz plain chocolate, broken into pieces**
- **125 g/4 oz unsalted butter or margarine**
- **250 g/8 oz caster sugar**
- **2 eggs**
- **300 g/10 oz self-raising flour**
- **1 teaspoon bicarbonate of soda**
- **2 tablespoons cocoa powder**

FILLING:
- **150 ml/¼ pint double cream**
- **1 quantity Almond Praline (see page 9)**

ICING:
- **250 g/8 oz plain chocolate, broken into pieces**
- **125 g/4 oz unsalted butter**
- **200 g/7 oz icing sugar**
- **5 tablespoons milk**
- **chocolate caraque (see page 24), to decorate**
- **icing sugar, for dusting**

1 Grease and line a 20 cm/8 inch round cake tin.

2 Mix together the milk and lemon juice. Put the chocolate in a heatproof bowl and leave over a saucepan of gently simmering water until it has melted.

3 Beat together the butter or margarine and sugar in a large bowl. Add the eggs and beat in. Sift the flour, bicarbonate of soda and cocoa powder into the bowl and mix well.

4 Add half the milk and lemon juice mixture and beat well. Stir in the melted chocolate and the remaining milk and beat until smooth. Turn into the prepared tin and level the surface.

5 Bake in a preheated oven for *1¼–1½ hours*, or until well risen and a skewer, inserted into the centre, comes out clean. Leave to cool in the tin.

6 Split the cake horizontally into 3 layers. Lightly whip the cream and stir in the praline. Use to sandwich the layers of cake together. Place on a serving plate.

7 To make the icing, put the chocolate in a heatproof bowl with the butter and leave over a saucepan of simmering water until melted. Stir once. Remove from the heat.

8 Add the icing sugar and milk, and beat until smooth. Leave the icing until cool enough to hold its shape.

9 Using a palette knife, spread the icing all over the top and sides of the cake. Scatter with chocolate caraque and serve dusted with icing sugar.

Makes one 3-layer 20cm/8 inch cake

Decadent Chocolate Tart

Preparation time: 20 minutes, plus cooling, chilling and setting
Cooking time: 20 minutes
Oven temperature: 200°C (400°F), Gas Mark 6

CITRUS SHORTCRUST PASTRY:
- 250 g/8 oz plain flour
- 125 g/4 oz unsalted butter
- 2 tablespoons caster sugar
- 1 tablespoon grated orange rind
- 1 tablespoon grated lemon rind
- iced water

FILLING:
- 250 ml/8 fl oz cream
- 300 g/10 oz plain chocolate, chopped
- 3 tablespoons espresso coffee liquid
- 4 tablespoons brandy
- chocolate shavings (see page 25), to decorate

1 To make the pastry, sift the flour into a bowl, add the butter cut into small pieces and rub in with the fingertips. Add the sugar and orange and lemon rinds and enough water to mix to a smooth dough. Knead lightly then press into a ball. Wrap in greaseproof paper or clingfilm and refrigerate for at least *30 minutes* before rolling.

2 Roll out the pastry on a lightly floured surface and use to line a 20 cm/8 inch square tart tin. Line with nonstick baking paper or greaseproof paper and fill with baking beans or rice.

3 Bake the tart case blind (see page 9) in a preheated oven, 200°C (400°F), Gas Mark 6, for *10 minutes*, then remove the beans or rice and paper and bake for a further *10 minutes* or until golden and cooked. Leave to cool.

4 To make the filling, place the cream in a saucepan and bring to the boil. Add the chocolate and stir until smooth. Remove from the heat and add the coffee and brandy.

5 Pour the filling into the pastry case and refrigerate until set.

6 Decorate the tart with chocolate shavings and serve in slices with cream.

Serves 6–8

Mud Pies

Preparation time: 25 minutes, plus chilling
Cooking time: 35 minutes
Oven temperature: 200°C (400°F), Gas Mark 6

- berries, to decorate

SWEET SHORTCRUST PASTRY:

- 250 g/8 oz plain flour

- 125 g/4 oz unsalted butter

- 2 tablespoons caster sugar

- iced water

FILLING:

- 75 g/3 oz unsalted butter

- 125 g/4 oz plain chocolate

- 90 g/3½ oz caster sugar

- 2 eggs, beaten

- 75 g/3 oz plain flour

1 To make the pastry, sift the flour into a bowl, add the butter cut into small pieces and rub in with the fingertips. Add the sugar and enough water to mix to a smooth dough. Knead lightly then press into a ball. Wrap in greaseproof paper or clingfilm and refrigerate for at least *30 minutes* before rolling.

2 Roll out the pastry and place in four 10 cm/4 inch pie tins. Line the pastry with nonstick baking paper or greaseproof paper and fill with baking beans or rice. Bake blind in a preheated oven, 200°C (400°F), Gas Mark 6, for *10 minutes*. Remove the beans or rice and paper and bake for a further *5 minutes* or until golden.

3 To make the filling, melt the butter and chocolate together over a low heat and stir in the sugar, eggs and flour.

4 Pour the filling into the pie cases. Reduce the oven heat to 180°C (350°F), Gas Mark 4 and bake for *20 minutes* or until cooked. Test with a warm skewer.

5 Decorate with blueberries or other berries and serve warm or cold with cream.

Makes 4 pies

Favourite Desserts

Seeking an attractive dessert to end a meal? You will find all you could wish for here, from winter warmers like Treacle Sponge to such summer delights as fruit fools and Lime Meringue Pie. If something classically impressive is needed, this chapter can provide that, too: Classic French Cheesecake, for instance, or the popular Italian dessert, Tiramisu.

Rhubarb Fool

Preparation time: 10 minutes, plus cooling
Cooking time: about 5 minutes

- I kg/2 lb young rhubarb
- 125–175 g/4–6 oz demerara
  sugar
- finely grated rind of 1 small
  orange
- 275 ml/9 fl oz double cream,
  softly whipped

- 2 teaspoons Pernod
  (optional)
- a little finely chopped
  preserved ginger in syrup, to
  decorate (optional)

1 Trim the rhubarb stalks of any leaves or brown roots. Chop the stalks into 5 cm/2 inch lengths and put them into a heavy saucepan with the sugar and orange rind and just a little water. Simmer for about *5 minutes*, or until the fruit is tender.

2 Drain the excess juice away then either sieve the fruit or purée it in a food processor, or leave it whole.

3 When cold, lightly stir in the cream and the Pernod, if using, aiming for a marbled effect. Serve the fool decorated with the preserved ginger, if liked.

Serves 4

variation
Light Rhubarb Fool

For a less rich dessert, stew the rhubarb as directed and serve it with soured cream or thick Greek yogurt sprinkled with a little demerara sugar.

Mango Fool

Preparation time: 15 minutes, plus chilling
Cooking time: 15–20 minutes

- 6 mangoes
- 125 g/4 oz sugar
- juice of ½ lime
- 150 ml/¼ pint water

- 1 egg
- 150 ml/¼ pint milk
- 125 ml/4 fl oz double cream

1 Peel the mangoes and cut out the stones. Chop the flesh into small pieces and place it in a saucepan with the sugar, lime juice and water. Simmer gently over a low heat until soft and pulpy.

2 Push the mango mixture through a sieve, and then beat the purée thoroughly until smooth. Cover and set aside to cool while you make the custard.

3 Break the egg into a bowl and beat lightly. Heat the milk to scalding point and then stir into the beaten egg. Return to the heat and stir constantly over a very low heat until the custard thickens. Do not allow it to boil.

4 Remove the custard from the heat and allow to cool. Stir in the mango purée and the cream. Do not blend thoroughly; the fool should look marbled. Pour into glasses or individual dishes and chill before serving.

Serves 6

Tiramisu

Preparation time: 20 minutes, plus chilling

- 2 egg yolks
- 2 tablespoons caster sugar
- few drops of vanilla extract
- 250 g/8 oz mascarpone cheese
- 175 ml/6 fl oz strong black coffee
- 2 tablespoons Marsala
- 1 tablespoon brandy
- 150 g/5 oz sponge fingers
- 1 tablespoon cocoa powder
- 2 tablespoons grated plain chocolate

1 Mix the egg yolks and sugar together in a bowl, beating with a wooden spoon until they are creamy. Add the vanilla and fold in the mascarpone. The mixture should be thick and creamy.

2 Mix the coffee with the Marsala and brandy in a bowl. Quickly dip the sponge fingers into the coffee mixture. They should absorb just enough liquid to flavour them without going soggy and falling apart.

3 Arrange some of the soaked sponge fingers in the base of a large attractive glass serving bowl or 6 individual serving dishes. Cover with a layer of the mascarpone mixture.

4 Continue layering alternately sponge fingers and mascarpone, finishing with a layer of mascarpone. Sift the cocoa over the top and sprinkle with the grated chocolate. Chill in the refrigerator for *3–4 hours* or until set. The flavour improves if the tiramisu is left overnight.

Serves 6

Lime Meringue Pie

Preparation time: 15 minutes, plus cooling
Cooking time: 45 minutes
Oven temperature: 200°C (400°F), Gas Mark 6

- **20 cm/8 inch shortcrust pastry case (see Tarte aux Poires, page 58)**

FILLING:
- **grated rind and juice of 3 limes**
- **175 g/6 oz caster sugar**

- **3 eggs, beaten**
- **250 g/8 oz butter, cut into small dice**

MERINGUE:
- **3 egg whites**
- **75 g/3 oz caster sugar**

1 Make the pastry dough as for Tarte aux Poires and use it to line a 20 cm/8 inch flan dish or tart tin. Prick the base lightly with a fork and bake blind (see page 9) in a preheated oven, 200°C (400°F), Gas Mark 6, for about *10 minutes*. Remove the pastry case from the oven and put it on a wire rack. Reduce the oven temperature to 190°C (375°F), Gas Mark 5.

2 To make the pie filling, put the grated lime rind and juice in a heavy-based saucepan with the caster sugar and eggs. Place over a very low heat and stir well.

3 Add the butter to the lime mixture in the pan, one cube at a time. Continue stirring all the time over a low heat, until all the butter has been incorporated and the mixture is hot.

4 Pour the lime mixture into the pastry case and bake in the centre of the preheated oven, 190°C (375°F), Gas Mark 5, for about *10 minutes*, or until the filling is just set. Remove the pie from the oven and leave to cool. Leave the oven on.

5 To make the meringue topping, whisk the egg whites until they stand in stiff peaks. Gradually beat in the caster sugar, a little at a time. Pile the meringue on top of the lime filling and bake for *12–15 minutes*, until the meringue is delicately browned. Meringue can brown very suddenly, so keep a close watch over it. Serve hot or cold.

Serves 6–8

Banana Rum Fritters

Preparation time: 15 minutes, plus standing
Cooking time: 10 minutes

- 4 large, ripe bananas
- 25 g/1 oz sugar
- 5 tablespoons dark rum
- oil, for deep-frying

TO SERVE:

- caster sugar
- ground cinnamon

BATTER:

- 75 g/3 oz plain flour
- pinch of salt
- 1 tablespoon olive oil
- 150 ml/¼ pint water
- 2 egg whites

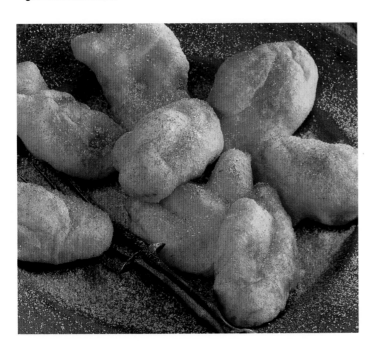

1 Peel the bananas and then cut them diagonally into slices, about 1 cm/½ inch thick. Place them in a shallow dish and sprinkle with the sugar. Pour the rum over the top and set aside for *1½ hours*, turning from time to time.

2 Meanwhile, make the batter. Sift the flour and salt together into a bowl. Make a well in the centre and gradually mix in the olive oil and water. Mix to a smooth batter and leave to stand for *1 hour*.

3 Just before the batter is needed, beat the egg whites stiffly and then lightly fold them into the batter. Drain the banana slices and dip them into the batter so that they are completely coated.

4 Heat the oil for deep-frying and when it is very hot, 190°C (375°F) or when a cube of day-old bread browns in *30 seconds*, fry the bananas, a few pieces at a time, until golden brown on both sides. Drain on absorbent kitchen paper. Serve the fritters really hot, sprinkled with caster sugar and cinnamon.

Serves 4

Classic French Cheesecake

Preparation time: 20 minutes, plus cooling
Cooking time: 50 minutes
Oven temperature: 180°C (350°F), Gas Mark 4

- 25 g/1 oz raisins
- 1 tablespoon Kirsch
- 250 g/8 oz Pâte Brisée (see page 8)
- 200 g/7 oz fromage blanc
- 3 tablespoons single cream
- 125 g/4 oz sugar
- 3 eggs, separated
- 15 g/½ oz arrowroot
- grated rind of 1 lemon
- icing sugar, for dusting

1 Put the raisins in a small bowl with the Kirsch. Leave to soak while you prepare the cheesecake.

2 Line a 23 cm/9 inch loose-bottomed flan tin with the pâte brisée. Prick the base with a fork.

3 Put the fromage blanc in a bowl and mix in the cream and sugar. Gently beat in the egg yolks, arrowroot and lemon rind. Whisk the egg whites until stiff and fold gently into the cream cheese mixture.

4 Pour the cream cheese filling into the pastry case. Sprinkle the surface of the tart with the soaked raisins.

5 Put the cheesecake in a preheated oven, 180°C (350°F), Gas Mark 4. After *10 minutes* lower the oven temperature to 150°C (300°F), Gas Mark 2, and bake for a further *40 minutes*. The cheesecake is cooked when the blade of a knife inserted into it comes out dry. Remove from the tin and cool. When cold, dust with icing sugar, and serve.

Serves 6

Treacle Sponge

Preparation time: 20 minutes
Cooking time: 1½ hours

- 125 g/4 oz butter
- 125 g/4 oz caster sugar
- grated rind of 1 orange
- 2 eggs, beaten
- 150 g/5 oz self-raising flour, sifted
- 4 tablespoons golden syrup

1 Grease a 900 ml/1½ pint pudding basin.

2 Cream the butter, sugar and orange rind together until they are light and fluffy.

3 Add the eggs gradually and beat well between each addition. Fold the flour into the mixture.

4 Spoon the syrup into the bottom of the pudding basin and pour the sponge mixture on top.

5 Cover the basin with a pleated piece of greased, greaseproof paper and aluminium foil large enough to allow for expansion and tie with string.

6 Place the basin in a heavy saucepan, two-thirds full of hot water, cover and steam steadily over a low heat for approximately *1½ hours*. Top up with hot water if necessary during the cooking time.

7 To serve, remove the string, paper and foil and turn the sponge out on to a warmed dish. Serve with cream or custard.

Serves 4–6

Toffee Apple Pudding

Preparation time: 15 minutes
Cooking time: 1 hour
Oven temperature: 180°C (350°F), Gas Mark 4

- 250 g/8 oz self-raising flour
- pinch of salt
- 125 g/4 oz shredded suet
- about 6 tablespoons water
- 50 g/2 oz butter, softened
- 125 g/4 oz soft brown sugar
- 750 g/1½ lb cooking apples, peeled, cored and thinly sliced

1 Sift the flour and salt into a basin. Stir in the suet and mix to a firm dough with water.

2 Mix the butter with half the sugar and spread over the base and sides of a 900 ml/1½ pint pie dish.

3 On a lightly floured surface, roll out half the pastry and use to line the pie dish. Do not trim the edges. Fill with half the apples and sprinkle with the remaining sugar. Add the remaining apples and press down gently.

4 Fold the pastry edges in towards the centre of the dish. Roll out the remaining pastry, brush lightly with water and place, damp side down, on the apples. Tuck in the edges.

5 Bake in a preheated oven, 180°C (350°F), Gas Mark 4, for about *1 hour* until the pastry is golden and the apples are tender when tested with a skewer. Leave for *5 minutes*, then turn out on to a warmed plate. Serve at once.

Serves 4–6

Blackberry and Apple Crumble

Preparation time: about 15 minutes
Cooking time: 40–50 minutes
Oven temperature: 180°C (350°F), Gas Mark 4

- 500 g/1 lb cooking apples, peeled, cored and chopped
- 50–125 g/2–4 oz sugar, to taste
- 5 cm/2 inch strip of lemon rind
- 500 g/1 lb blackberries
- 125 g/4 oz flour, or 75 g/3 oz flour and 2 tablespoons muesli
- 125 g/4 oz demerara sugar
- 50 g/2 oz ground almonds
- 125 g/4 oz butter

1 Put the apples into a saucepan with a splash of water and cook gently with a little sugar and the lemon rind.

2 When the apples are softened, add the blackberries and simmer very gently until they are heated through.

3 Put the fruit into a pie dish, keeping back any excess juice: the mixture should not be too wet.

4 Rub together the flour (and muesli, if using), demerara sugar, ground almonds and butter for the crumble until you have a mixture with the texture of breadcrumbs.

5 Sprinkle the crumble mixture over the fruit and bake in a preheated oven, 180°C (350°F), Gas Mark 4, for *30 minutes* until the crumble is browned and crisp. If serving with whipped cream, add some of the reserved juice as you beat the cream, to flavour and colour it a little.

Serves 4–6

variation
Rhubarb and Orange Crumble

Cook the rhubarb in the same way as the apples in the main recipe, adding a little more sugar. Add the grated rind of 1 orange instead of the blackberries. Proceed as in the main recipe.

Pâtisserie

Sweet pastries, the high point of the pastry chef's art, are well within the home cook's reach via the easy-to-make recipes in this chapter. Fruits, nuts, chocolate and many other sweet recipe ingredients are brought into use, combined with all kinds of pastry to make a dazzling array of pâtisserie, including such favourites as Chocolate Eclairs, Plum Tart and a traditional apple pie from Normandy.

Tarte aux Pommes à la Normande

Preparation time: 35 minutes
Cooking time: 35–40 minutes
Oven temperature: 200°C (400°F), Gas Mark 6

- 75 g/3 oz butter
- 75 g/3 oz caster sugar
- 1 egg, beaten
- 75 g/3 oz ground almonds
- 1½ tablespoons plain flour, sifted
- 1 tablespoon Kirsch or rum

- 175 g/6 oz Pâte Brisée (see page 8)
- 3 dessert apples

TO DECORATE:

- icing sugar, for sprinkling
- apricot jam, sieved

1 To make the filling, cream the butter and sugar together until light and fluffy. Beat in the egg, a little at a time, then fold in the ground almonds, flour and Kirsch or rum.

2 Roll out the pastry into a circle and use to line a 23 cm/ 9 inch flan ring or flan dish. Trim the edges.

3 Pour the filling into the pastry case and smooth the surface.

4 Peel, halve and core the apples. Cut each apple half across into slices. Keeping each cut apple half together, slide a knife under to lift it and place it carefully on the filling in the pastry case. Slide the slices slightly apart and press them down into the filling.

5 Put the tart in a preheated oven, 200°C (400°F), Gas Mark 6, and bake for *15 minutes*. Reduce the oven temperature to 190°C (375°F), Gas Mark 5 and continue cooking for a further *10 minutes*. Sprinkle with a little sifted icing sugar and return to the oven for about *10 minutes*; the apples should be tender and the filling pleasantly coloured.

6 Remove from the oven, take off the flan ring, if using, and cool on a wire rack. Warm the apricot jam and add a little water if needed. Brush this glaze over the flan. The flan keeps for up to 2 days in a cool place.

Serves 8

Rhubarb Tart

Preparation time: 25–30 minutes, plus standing
Cooking time: 40 minutes
Oven temperature: 200°C (400°F), Gas Mark 6

- **500 g/1 lb rhubarb, thickly**
  sliced

PASTRY CASE:

- **1 quantity Raspberry and**
  Blueberry Tart pastry (see
  page 60)

GLAZE:

- **2 tablespoons redcurrant**
  jelly
- **1 tablespoon water**

FILLING:

- **175 g/6 oz sugar**
- **2 eggs**
- **50 g/2 oz plain flour**
- **grated rind of 1 orange**
- **150 ml/¼ pint double cream**

1 The day before you want to make the tart, sprinkle the rhubarb with half the sugar and leave to stand overnight.

2 Roll out the pastry and use to line a 20 cm/8 inch flan dish or tart tin, as in Raspberry and Blueberry Tart.

3 Bake the pastry case blind (see page 9) in a preheated oven, 200°C (400°F), Gas Mark 6, for about *10 minutes*, until the pastry has begun to form a slight crust. Remove the pastry case from the oven but leave the oven on.

4 To make the filling, mix together the eggs and the remaining sugar in a bowl. Add the flour and orange rind and then stir in the cream.

5 Spoon the rhubarb into the pastry case and cover with the filling. Return the tart to the oven for *30 minutes*.

6 Melt the redcurrant jelly with the water and use to brush over the tart while it is still hot. Serve hot or cold.

Serves 6

Apple Strip Tart

Preparation time: 25 minutes
Cooking time: 20 minutes
Oven temperature: 200°C (400°F), Gas Mark 6

- 250 g/8 oz frozen puff pastry, thawed
- flour, for sprinkling
- 1 egg yolk, beaten
- 1 kg/2 lb apples
- 2 tablespoons water
- 1 tablespoon lemon juice
- 1 quantity Crème Patissière (see page 8)

GLAZE:
- 3 tablespoons apricot jam
- 1 tablespoon water

1 Roll out the pastry into a rectangle 12 cm/5 inches wide. Sprinkle lightly with flour and fold in half lengthways. Cut a 1 cm/½ inch band from around the three open edges. Open out the rectangle and roll again so that it is 2 cm/1 inch wider and longer. Place on a dampened baking sheet, prick with a fork and dampen the edges. Open the band of pastry and press on to the rectangle to make a border. Brush the border with a little beaten egg yolk.

2 Bake the pastry in a preheated oven, 200°C (400°F), Gas Mark 6, for *10 minutes*. Take it out of the oven and reduce the oven temperature to 180°C (350°F), Gas Mark 4.

3 Peel and slice the apples thinly. Cook a quarter of them with the water until they have formed a smooth purée. Meanwhile, prevent the uncooked apple slices from turning brown by turning them in the lemon juice.

4 Spread the crème patissière evenly over the cooked pastry base. Cover this with a layer of apple purée, then arrange the apple slices in a fish scale pattern over the purée, starting at the centre and working out. Brush the pastry edges with the leftover egg yolk.

5 Return the tart to the oven and bake for a further *10 minutes*.

6 In a small pan, melt the apricot jam in the water then boil until smooth, stirring with a wooden spoon. Brush this glaze over the apple slices. Serve the tart hot or cold.

Serves 4–6

variation
Apricot Tart

Replace the apples with fresh apricots. Take care when making the apricot purée: the apricots should not be too watery or overcooked. Omit the lemon juice and halve the apricots rather than slicing them. Proceed as for the main recipe.

Twelfth Night Frangipane Cake

Preparation time: 25–30 minutes
Cooking time: 20 minutes
Oven temperature: 220°C (425°F), Gas Mark 7

- 90 g/3½ oz ground almonds
- 90 g/3½ oz icing sugar, sifted
- 1 whole egg and 1 egg yolk
- 50 g/2 oz butter, softened

- 2 tablespoons Cointreau
- 425 g/14 oz frozen puff
  pastry, thawed
- 2 china beans or silver coins

1 To make the frangipane, beat together the ground almonds, sugar, whole egg, softened butter and Cointreau.

2 Roll out the pastry on a floured surface into a rectangle. Cut two circles out of the pastry, using a 20 cm/8 inch flan dish or tart tin as a template. Make one circle the size of the dish, the other 2.5 cm/1 inch larger.

3 Butter the same flan dish or tart tin and line it with the larger circle of pastry. Spread the frangipane over the pastry. Hide the china beans or coins in the mixture. Wet the edges of the pastry with a little water and place the remaining circle on top. Seal the pastry by pressing the edges together.

4 Beat the remaining egg yolk with a little water and brush it over the surface of the cake. Make a lattice pattern on the top with the back of a knife.

5 Bake the cake in a preheated oven, 220°C (425°F), Gas Mark 7, for *20 minutes*. The cake may be served hot or cold.

Serves 4–6

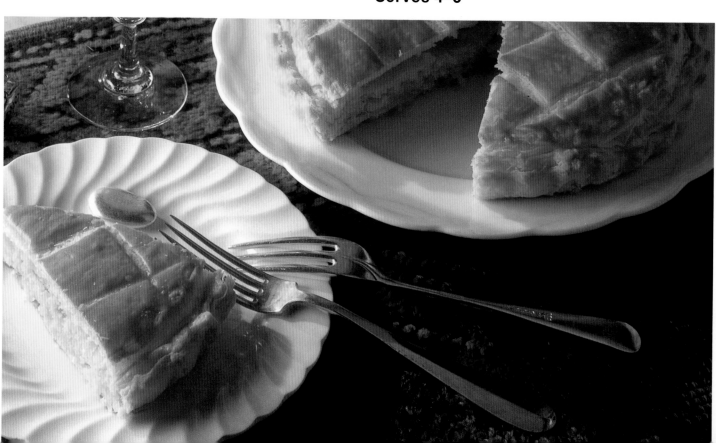

Passionfruit Curd Tart

Passionfruit are available all year round. Their sweet pulp is delicious and quite decorative.

Preparation time: 20 minutes, plus chilling
Cooking time: 25–30 minutes
Oven temperature: 200°C (400°F), Gas Mark 6

CITRUS SHORTCRUST PASTRY:
- 250 g/8 oz plain flour
- 125 g/4 oz unsalted butter
- 2 tablespoons caster sugar
- 1 tablespoon grated orange rind
- 1 tablespoon grated lemon rind
- iced water

FILLING:
- pulp of 6 passionfruit
- 200 g/7 oz caster sugar
- 125 ml/4 fl oz orange juice
- 2 teaspoons grated orange rind
- 4 eggs
- 175 ml/6 fl oz cream
- icing sugar, for sprinkling

1 To make the pastry, sift the flour into a bowl, add the butter cut into small pieces and rub in with the fingertips. Add the sugar and orange and lemon rinds and enough iced water to mix to a smooth dough. Knead lightly then press into a ball. Wrap in greaseproof paper or clingfilm and refrigerate for at least *30 minutes* before rolling out.

2 Roll out the pastry on a lightly floured surface and use to line a 12 x 25 cm/5 x 10 inch rectangular tart tin. Line with nonstick baking paper or greaseproof paper and fill with baking beans or rice. Bake in a preheated oven, 200°C (400°F), Gas Mark 6, for *10 minutes*, then remove the beans or rice and paper.

3 To make the filling, mix the passionfruit pulp with the sugar, orange juice and rind, eggs and cream.

4 Pour the filling into the tart case. Reduce the oven temperature to 190°C (375°F), Gas Mark 5 and bake for *15–20 minutes* or until the filling is firm. Sprinkle the tart with icing sugar and place under a hot grill until the sugar has melted and is golden brown.

5 Serve in slices with crème fraîche.

Serves 8

Tarte aux Poires

Preparation time: 20–25 minutes, plus chilling
Cooking time: 50 minutes
Oven temperature: 200°C (400°F), Gas Mark 6

PASTRY:

- **200 g/7 oz plain flour**
- **pinch of salt**
- **90 g/3½ oz butter**
- **3 tablespoons cold milk (or water, if preferred)**

FILLING:

- **250 ml/8 fl oz double cream**
- **2 egg yolks**
- **2 tablespoons caster sugar**
- **1 tablespoon Calvados or sherry**
- **4 large ripe, but firm pears, peeled**

1 To make the pastry, sift the flour and salt into a bowl. Dice the butter into the flour and rub in, then mix to a dough with the milk. Leave to rest in the refrigerator for *20 minutes*.

2 Roll out the chilled dough on a floured surface and use it to line a lightly greased deep 20 cm/8 inch flan dish or tart tin. Prick the base lightly with a fork and bake blind (see page 9) for about *10 minutes*, until the pastry has begun to form a slight crust. Take the tart case out of the oven and put it on a wire rack. Leave the oven turned on.

3 To make the filling, beat together the cream, egg yolks, sugar and Calvados or sherry.

4 Halve the pears and remove the cores with a teaspoon. Make vertical slices in the pear halves without cutting all the way through. Place them, flat sides down, in the pastry case. Cover the pears with the filling and return the tart to the oven for *40 minutes*. Serve warm or cold with single cream.

Serves 6

Raspberry and Blueberry Tart

Preparation time: 25 minutes
Cooking time: 35 minutes
Oven temperature: 190°C (375°F), Gas Mark 5

PASTRY:
- 200 g/7 oz plain flour
- pinch of salt
- 90 g/3½ oz butter
- 3 tablespoons cold water

FILLING:
- 125 g/4 oz sugar
- 150 ml/¼ pint double cream
- 2 eggs, beaten
- 1 tablespoon Myrte liqueur (optional)
- 250 g/8 oz blueberries
- 250 g/8 oz raspberries, hulled

1 To make the pastry, sift the flour and salt into a bowl. Dice the butter into the flour and rub in, then mix to a dough with the water. Roll out the dough on a floured surface and use it to line a buttered 20 cm/8 inch flan dish or tart tin. Prick the base lightly with a fork.

2 To make the filling, mix together all but 1 tablespoon of the sugar, the cream, beaten eggs and liqueur, if using. Pour the mixture into the unbaked pastry case.

3 Bake the tart in a preheated oven, 190°C (375°F), Gas Mark 5, for *25 minutes* then remove from the oven.

4 Arrange the freshly prepared fruit on top and sprinkle over the remaining sugar. Return the tart to the oven for a further *10 minutes*. Serve hot or cold.

Serves 4–6

variation

Blackcurrant Tart

Replace the blueberries and raspberries with the same weight of blackcurrants (or blackcurrants and redcurrants). Replace the Myrte liqueur with the blackcurrant liqueur, crème de Cassis, if you want the extra tang of a liqueur in the tart.

Plum Tart

Preparation time: 25 minutes, plus chilling
Cooking time: 55 minutes
Oven temperature: 200°C (400°F), Gas Mark 6

PASTRY:

- 175 g/6 oz plain flour
- 2 tablespoons icing sugar
- 65 g/2½ oz unsalted butter,
  cut into pieces
- 1 egg, lightly beaten
- 2–3 tablespoons water

FILLING:

- 400 g/13 oz can dark plums,
  drained
- 65 g/2½ oz unsalted butter,
  chopped
- 175 g/6 oz brown sugar
- 325 g/11 oz ground
  hazelnuts
- 3 eggs, separated

1 To make the pastry, sift the flour and icing sugar into a mixing bowl and rub in the butter with your fingertips until the mixture resembles fine breadcrumbs. Add the egg and water and combine until the mixture forms a ball.

2 Turn out the pastry on to a lightly floured surface and knead very gently, just until smooth underneath. Wrap in clingfilm and chill for *15 minutes*. Roll out the pastry and line a 25 cm/10 inch flan tin. Cut a piece of greaseproof paper large enough to cover the pastry, place in the pastry case and spread with a layer of baking beans or rice and bake blind in a preheated oven, 200°C (400°F), Gas Mark 6, for *10 minutes*. Remove the paper and beans or rice and bake for a further *5 minutes*. Remove and cool slightly. Reduce the oven temperature to 180°C (350°F), Gas Mark 4.

3 To make the filling, cover the base of the tart with the well drained plums. Beat the butter and sugar together until pale and creamy. Fold in the hazelnuts and egg yolks. Whisk the egg whites until soft peaks form. Fold into the hazelnut mixture. Spoon over plums. Bake for *40 minutes* or until set. Serve with whipped cream.

Serves 6–8

Chocolate Eclairs

Preparation time: 25 minutes, plus cooling
Cooking time: 35 minutes
Oven temperature: 200°C (400°F), Gas Mark 6

CHOUX PASTRY:
- 65 g/2½ oz plain flour
- 50 g/2 oz lightly salted butter
- 150 ml/¼ pint cold water
- 2 eggs, beaten

TO FINISH:
- 300 ml/½ pint double cream
- 1 tablespoon icing sugar
- 125 g/4 oz plain chocolate, broken into pieces
- 40 g/1½ oz white chocolate, broken into pieces

1 To make the choux pastry, sift the flour on to greaseproof paper. Put the butter in a small saucepan with the water and heat gently until the butter melts. Bring to the boil and remove from the heat.

2 Immediately tip in the flour and beat until the mixture forms a ball, which comes away from the sides of the pan. Leave to cool for *3 minutes*.

3 Gradually beat the eggs into the dough, a little at a time, until it is glossy.

4 Lightly grease, then dampen a large baking sheet. Put the dough into a large piping bag fitted with a 1 cm/½ inch plain nozzle. Pipe the dough in 7.5 cm/3 inch fingers on to the baking sheet. Alternatively, if you prefer, you can use a teaspoon to place similar-sized lengths of dough on the baking sheet.

5 Bake in a preheated oven, 200°C (400°F) Gas Mark 6, for about *35 minutes* until well-risen, crisp and golden. Make a slit down the side of each éclair to release the steam, then transfer to a wire rack to cool.

6 Whip the cream with the icing sugar until the mixture just forms soft peaks. Spoon or pipe into the éclairs.

7 Melt the plain and white chocolates in separate bowls over saucepans of simmering water. Spread a little plain chocolate over each éclair, then spoon a little white chocolate over the plain chocolate swirling it into a pattern with a spoon or cocktail stick. Leave the chocolate to set lightly before serving the éclairs.

Makes about 14

Fresh Strawberry and Almond Tartlets

Preparation time: 30 minutes, plus chilling and setting
Cooking time: about 20 minutes
Oven temperature: 190°C (375°F), Gas Mark 5

- 250 g/8 oz butter
- 125 g/4 oz caster sugar
- 2 egg yolks
- 375 g/12 oz plain flour, sifted
- 125 g/4 oz ground almonds

FILLING:

- 250 g/8 oz full-fat soft
  cheese
- 1 tablespoon caster sugar
- 1 teaspoon finely grated
  lemon rind
- 750 g/1½ lb strawberries
- 5 tablespoons redcurrant
  jelly, melted
- 4 tablespoons blanched
  almonds, toasted

1 Cream the butter and sugar together in a bowl until light and fluffy. Beat in the egg yolks. Gradually stir in the flour and ground almonds, and knead to a smooth dough. Cover with clingfilm or foil and chill for *1 hour*.

2 Divide the dough into 8 or 16 pieces. Roll out each one into a round and use to line 8 greased 11 cm/4½ inch individual tartlet or Yorkshire pudding tins or 16 smaller tartlet tins. Prick the surface of the pastry cases all over with a fork.

3 Put the pastry cases in a preheated oven, 190°C (375°F), Gas Mark 5, and bake blind (see page 9) for *15 minutes*. Remove the foil and beans used for the blind baking and return the pastry cases to the oven for a further *3–4 minutes* or until golden brown. Let the pastry cases cool in the tins on a wire rack.

4 To make the filling, beat together the cheese, sugar and lemon rind. Spread a little of the cheese mixture in each pastry case.

5 Reserve 8 or 16 of the best strawberries. Hull and slice the remainder. Arrange the strawberry slices in rings in the pastry cases. Spoon the redcurrant jelly over the strawberries and leave to set.

6 Just before serving, top with the reserved strawberries and scatter over the toasted almonds.

Serves 8

variation _____

Raspberry and Amaretti Tartlets

Replace the sliced strawberries with whole raspberries. Replace the filling with 300 ml/½ pint whipped double cream folded together with 10 crushed amaretti biscuits.

Biscuits and Cakes

A biscuit or two, a slice of cake, something to drink with them: it is the perfect recipe for a morning or afternoon break. There are all sorts of cakes and biscuits here, from splendidly iced and decorated layer cakes and gâteaux to a no-cook chocolate cake and ginger biscuits. You will find something for every occasion, from a simple pause in the day's work to a formal tea party.

No-cook Chocolate Nut Slice

Preparation time: 15 minutes, plus chilling

- edible rice paper
- 375 g/12 oz plain chocolate, broken into pieces
- 175 g/6 oz unsalted butter
- 125 g/4 oz digestive biscuits, chopped into small pieces
- 175 g/6 oz mixed whole nuts, e.g. almonds, hazelnuts or Brazil nuts

1 Line the base and 2 cm/¾ inch up the sides of an 18 cm/ 7 inch square shallow baking tin or cake tin with the rice paper.

2 Put the chocolate and butter into a heatproof bowl over a pan of simmering water and leave until melted.

3 Stir in the biscuits and nuts then turn into the prepared tin. Spread the mixture evenly then chill for several hours or overnight until firm.

4 To serve, remove the cake from the tin and cut or break it into small pieces.

Makes 14–16

Ginger Shortbread

Preparation time: 20 minutes
Cooking time: 15–20 minutes
Oven temperature: 160°C (325°F), Gas Mark 3

- 250 g/8 oz butter, softened
- 125 g/4 oz caster sugar
- 250 g/8 oz plain flour, sifted
- 2 teaspoons ground ginger
- caster sugar, for sprinkling

1 Cream together the butter and sugar on a clean surface. Gradually work in the sifted flour and ginger to form a dough. Knead until smooth.

2 Roll out the dough on a lightly floured surface to 5 mm/ ¼ inch thick and cut into rounds with a medium scone cutter, which would give about 36 biscuits, or any fancy shaped cutter. Place on a greased baking sheet.

3 Bake in a preheated oven, 160°C (325°F), Gas Mark 3, for *15–20 minutes*, or until golden brown. Sprinkle with caster sugar while still warm. Cool the biscuits on a wire rack.

Makes about 36

variation
Gingerbread Men

Though not the standard recipe, this one is good for gingerbread men, provided the cutter you use is not too large. Press currants into the face for eyes before baking.

Florentine Slices

Preparation time: 25 minutes, plus setting and cooling
Cooking time: 40–45 minutes
Oven temperature: 150°C (300°F), Gas Mark 2

- 250 g/8 oz plain chocolate, broken into pieces
- 50 g/2 oz butter
- 125 g/4 oz demerara sugar
- 1 egg, beaten
- 50 g/2 oz mixed dried fruit
- 125 g/4 oz desiccated coconut
- 50 g/2 oz chopped mixed peel or glacé cherries, quartered

1 Grease a 19 cm/7½ inch square cake tin.

2 Put the chocolate pieces in a heatproof bowl and place over a pan of hot water until melted, stirring occasionally. Spoon the chocolate into the prepared tin. Spread it out evenly over the bottom and leave to set.

3 Meanwhile, cream together the butter and sugar until the mixture is light and fluffy. Beat in the egg thoroughly. Mix together the remaining ingredients and add to the creamed mixture. Spoon into the tin and spread over the set chocolate.

4 Bake in the centre of a preheated oven, 150°C (300°F), Gas Mark 2, for *40–45 minutes*, or until golden brown. Remove from the oven and leave for *5 minutes*, then carefully mark into 12–16 squares with a sharp knife. The mixture will be quite sticky at this stage.

5 Leave until cold, then loosen with a palette knife and lift each square carefully from the tin so as not to mark the chocolate.

Makes 12–16

Banana Cake

Preparation time: 20 minutes, plus cooling
Cooking time: 20–25 minutes
Oven temperature: 180°C (350°F), Gas Mark 4

- 125 g/4 oz butter or
  margarine
- 125 g/4 oz caster sugar
- 2 eggs
- 125 g/4 oz self-raising flour,
  sifted
- 2 bananas, mashed

- icing sugar, for dredging

FILLING:

- 50 g/2 oz ground almonds
- 50 g/2 oz icing sugar, sifted
- 1 small banana, mashed
- ½ teaspoon lemon juice

1 Cream together the butter or margarine and sugar until light and fluffy. Add the eggs one at a time, adding a tablespoon of flour with the second egg. Fold in the remaining flour with the bananas.

2 Divide the mixture between two 18 cm/7 inch lined and greased sandwich tins. Bake in a preheated oven, 180°C (350°F), Gas Mark 4, for *20–25 minutes* until the cakes spring back when lightly pressed. Turn on to a wire rack to cool.

3 To make the filling, mix the ground almonds with the icing sugar, then add the banana and lemon juice and mix to a smooth paste. Sandwich the cakes together with the filling and dredge with icing sugar.

Makes one 18 cm/7 inch cake

Finishing touches

Decorating your sweet treats does not have to be complicated. There are a lot of fruits, nuts and even fresh flowers and herbs – many of which are shown here – that can be used to add decorative touches to cakes, puddings and desserts. Some of these need to be frosted first with sugar but other than that they need nothing more to make them both look and taste extra special.

Frosted rose petals

Frosted mint leaves

Frosted primula flowers

Frosted black grapes

Frosted green grapes

Frosted physalis

Frosted primula flowers are easy to make. Lightly whisk an egg white and, using a paint brush, lightly coat the petals, draining off any excess. Dip or dredge in caster sugar. Place on greaseproof paper to dry. Store between layers of tissue paper in an airtight container for up to six weeks.

Frosted rose petals Make these in exactly the same way.

Frosted black grapes Frost and store in an airtight container for up to two weeks.

Frosted mint leaves These taste as good as they look.

Frosted physalis is one of the most attractive fruits.

Frosted green grapes work as well as black ones.

Redcurrants Small fruits all work equally well and these look especially effective.

Shredded rind Use a potato peeler to pare the rind from a citrus fruit, then arrange as twists or cut into thin shreds. Alternatively, use a canelle knife to make shreds.

Almonds may be toasted before use. They are available

unblanched or blanched, and whole, chopped, sliced, flaked or slivered. Buy as fresh as possible and store unshelled for up to six months in a cool place, and shelled for several months in the fridge or six months in the freezer.

Hazelnuts, also known as filberts, have a pale gold flesh with a rich buttery flavour. They are available whole, halved, chopped or ground, and are best toasted before use. Store unshelled nuts in a cool dry place for up to six months, and shelled in the fridge for up to one month or in the freezer for six months.

Walnuts may be toasted before use. They can be stored unshelled in a cool dry place for several months, and shelled in the fridge for about two months or in the freezer for up to a year.

Pecan nuts are similar to walnuts. Use unshelled within six months. Store shelled in the fridge for up to three months, or in the freezer for six months.

Frosted redcurrants

Toasted hazelnuts

Halved hazelnuts

Walnuts

Chopped hazelnuts

Pecan nuts

Toasted blanched almonds

Slivered almonds

Shredded citrus rind

Orange rind twist

Toasted flaked almonds

Passion Cake

Preparation time: 20 minutes
Cooking time: 1 hour
Oven temperature: 180°C (350°F), Gas Mark 4

- 150 g/5 oz butter
- 200 g/7 oz soft light brown
  sugar
- 175 g/6 oz grated carrots
- ½ teaspoon salt
- 1 teaspoon ground mixed
  spice
- 2 eggs
- 200 g/7 oz self-raising flour
- 2 teaspoons baking powder
- 125 g/4 oz shelled walnuts,
  finely chopped

ICING:
- 250 g/8 oz full fat soft
  cheese
- 2–3 tablespoons lemon juice
- 50 g/2 oz icing sugar, sifted

TO FINISH:
- 25 g/1 oz shelled walnuts,
  halved

1 Grease a 20 cm/8 inch round cake tin and line with greased greaseproof paper.

2 Melt the butter and pour into a mixing bowl. Beat in the sugar, carrots, salt, mixed spice and eggs.

3 Sift the flour and baking powder together and add the walnuts. Lightly fold into the carrot mixture until evenly mixed.

4 Pour the mixture into the prepared tin. Bake in a preheated oven, 180°C (350°F), Gas Mark 4, for *1 hour*, until firm to the touch and golden brown.

5 Cool in the tin for *5 minutes*, then turn out and cool completely on a wire rack.

6 To make the icing, beat the cheese until smooth. Gradually beat in the lemon juice to taste, then beat in the icing sugar until well mixed.

7 Split the cake into two layers and sandwich the layers with one-third of the icing. Spread the remaining icing over the top and sides of the cake and mark wavy lines in it with a fork.

8 Sprinkle the top edge of the cake with the walnuts.

Serves 8

variation
Individual Passion Cakes

Preparation time: 25 minutes
Cooking time: 20–25 minutes

For individual passion cakes, bake the cake mixture in paper cake cases. The above quantity will make about 24 small cakes. Half fill the cases, then bake them in a preheated oven, 180°C (350°F), Gas Mark 4, for *20–25 minutes*. When cool, spread them with the cheese icing and top each one with a walnut half.

Coffee and Walnut Layer Cake

Preparation time: 35 minutes, plus cooling
Cooking time: 30–35 minutes
Oven temperature: 190°C (375°F), Gas Mark 5

- 4 eggs
- 175 g/6 oz caster sugar
- 125 g/4 oz plain flour, sifted
- 1 tablespoon oil
- 125 g/4 oz walnuts, finely chopped

BUTTER ICING:

- 250 g/8 oz butter
- 500 g/1 lb icing sugar, sifted
- 2 tablespoons milk
- 2 tablespoons coffee essence

TO DECORATE:

- walnut halves

1 Line and grease two 20 cm/8 inch sandwich tins. Whisk the eggs and sugar in a bowl over a pan of boiling water until thick enough to leave a trail. (If using an electric mixer, the hot water is unnecessary.)

2 Partially fold in the flour, then add the oil and chopped walnuts and fold in gently. Divide between the prepared tins and bake in a preheated oven, 190°C (375°F), Gas Mark 5, for *30–35 minutes* until the cakes spring back when lightly pressed. Turn on to a wire rack to cool. Split each cake in half.

3 To make the butter icing, cream the butter with half the icing sugar until soft, then add the milk, coffee essence and the remaining icing sugar. Beat well.

4 Divide a quarter of the icing between each of three cake rounds and sandwich the cake together. Swirl the remaining icing over the top and sides of the assembled cake and decorate with walnut halves.

Makes one 20 cm/8 inch cake

Lemon Cream Sponge

Preparation time: 30 minutes, plus cooling
Cooking time: 20 minutes
Oven temperature: 180°C (350°F), Gas Mark 4

- **3 eggs**
- **75 g/3 oz caster sugar**
- **75 g/3 oz self-raising flour**
- **150 ml/¼ pint double cream, lightly whipped**
- **2 tablespoons lemon curd**

TO DECORATE:
- **sifted icing sugar**
- **shredded lemon rind**
- **twisted lemon slices**

1 Grease two 18 cm/7 inch sandwich tins and line them with greased greaseproof paper.

2 Put the eggs and sugar in a heatproof bowl over a pan of hot water and whisk until the mixture is thick and creamy. Remove from the heat and whisk for a further *2 minutes*. (If using an electric mixer, no heat is needed.) Sift in the flour and carefully fold it in.

3 Divide the mixture between the tins and bake in a preheated oven, 180°C (350°F), Gas Mark 4, for *20 minutes*, or until the tops spring back when lightly pressed with the fingertips. Turn out on to a wire rack to cool.

4 Mix the cream with the lemon curd and use to sandwich the cooled cakes together. Dredge the top of the cake with icing sugar and decorate with shredded lemon rind and twisted lemon slices.

Makes one 18 cm/7 inch cake

Moist Apple-spice Cake

Preparation time: 40 minutes, plus cooling
Cooking time: 1¼ hours
Oven temperature: 180°C (350°F), Gas Mark 4

- 300 g/10 oz self-raising flour
- 1 teaspoon salt
- ½ teaspoon ground cinnamon
- ¼ teaspoon ground cloves
- 125 g/4 oz butter, softened
- 250 g/8 oz caster sugar
- 1 egg, lightly beaten

- 1 teaspoon vanilla essence
- 375 g/12 oz cooking apples, peeled, cored and grated
- 1 tablespoon clear honey
- 2–3 tablespoons toasted flaked almonds

1 Grease an 18 cm/7 inch square cake tin and line with greased greaseproof paper.

2 Sift the flour with the salt and ground cinnamon and cloves twice. Cream the butter and sugar together until pale and fluffy. Gradually beat in the egg and vanilla essence. Stir in the apples and fold in the flour.

3 Turn the mixture into the prepared tin and smooth the top. Bake in a preheated oven, 180°C (350°F), Gas Mark 4, for *1¼ hours* or until the cake is lightly browned and the sides are shrinking from the tin. Leave in the tin for *5 minutes*, then turn out on to a wire rack to cool.

4 Remove the greaseproof paper from the cooled cake. Brush the top with honey and arrange the nuts on top.

Makes one 18 cm/7 inch square cake

Strawberry Cake

For a professional finish, brush the strawberries that are used for the decoration with a little warmed redcurrant jelly or sieved strawberry jam. This gives them an attractive sheen and intensifies the colour of the berries.

Preparation time: 1 hour, plus cooling
Cooking time: 30 minutes
Oven temperature: 180°C (350°F), Gas Mark 4

- 200 g/7 oz caster sugar
- 2 teaspoons grated lemon rind
- 5 eggs, separated
- 50 ml/2 fl oz boiling water
- 2 tablespoons lemon juice
- 175 g/6 oz self-raising flour
- 350 ml/12 fl oz double cream
- ½ teaspoon vanilla essence
- 1 tablespoon icing sugar
- 500 g/1 lb strawberries, washed and hulled

1 Grease and flour two 20 cm/8 inch square cake tins.

2 Stir together the sugar and lemon rind. Set the egg whites aside and beat the egg yolks until pale, then gradually beat in the sugar. When very thick and creamy, stir in the boiling water and lemon juice.

3 Sift the flour twice, then sift it over the top of the egg yolk mixture. Fold in lightly but thoroughly.

4 Whip the egg whites until thick and fold in lightly. Divide the mixture evenly between the tins. Bake in a preheated oven, 180°C (350°F), Gas Mark 4, for *30 minutes*, or until the tops spring back when touched. Turn out on to wire racks to cool.

5 Whip the cream with the vanilla and icing sugar until stiff. Chop most of the strawberries and fold into three-quarters of the cream. Reserve the remaining cream and some whole strawberries for decoration.

6 With a sharp knife, carefully cut both cakes through the centre making four layers. Sandwich the layers together with strawberry cream. Pipe the reserved cream in a trellis pattern over the top, and decorate with whole strawberries.

Makes one 20 cm/8 inch square cake

Sweet Gifts

What better gift for friends and family than a box of mouth-wateringly gorgeous truffles, or a pretty pack of biscuits, nougat or chocolate Brazils. And, of course, they all give extra pleasure because they were made at home. You will find exciting recipes for all these sweet gifts, and others, in this chapter.

Nougat

Preparation time: 15 minutes, plus cooling
Cooking time: about 30 minutes
Oven temperature: 160°C (325°F), Gas Mark 3

- edible rice paper
- 125 g/4 oz blanched almonds, sliced into 2 or 3
- 15 g/½ oz pistachio nuts, blanched and halved (optional)
- 150 g/5 oz icing sugar, sifted
- 125 g/4 oz clear honey
- 25 g/1 oz powdered glucose
- 2 egg whites
- 50 g/2 oz glacé cherries, sliced
- 4 tablespoons icing sugar, sifted

1 Line the bottom and sides of an 18 cm/7 inch square tin with rice paper.

2 Spread the almonds and pistachio nuts, if using, on a baking sheet. Put them in a preheated oven, 160°C (325°F), Gas Mark 3, for about *5 minutes* to dry, then switch off the heat but leave the nuts in the oven to keep them warm.

3 Put the icing sugar, honey, glucose and egg whites into a fairly large heavy-based saucepan, preferably one with a curved side where it joins the base – a large milk saucepan is ideal. Place over a gentle heat and cook, beating well, until the mixture is thick and glossy and when a little of the mixture dropped into cold water forms a firm, but not hard, ball. This will take *20–30 minutes*. An electric hand whisk can be used at high speed until the mixture thickens, then slow down to a medium speed, or beat with a large wooden spoon.

4 Add the warm nuts and the cherries to the mixture. Mix well and turn out on to a board sprinkled with most of the sifted icing sugar. Leave to cool for *5–10 minutes,* sprinkle a little icing sugar over the top and then press the mixture out flat, to about the size of the prepared tin. Place it in the tin and flatten the mixture evenly. Cover with rice paper. Place a piece of cardboard on top, cut to the tin's shape, and weight it down – a large can is about the right weight.

5 Leave the nougat to cool, then cut it into small bars or squares and wrap in rice paper or waxed paper. The nougat will keep for up to 4 weeks in an airtight tin.

Makes about 500 g/1 lb

Chocolate Liqueur Cups

Preparation time: 45 minutes, plus chilling

CHOCOLATE CASES:

- 150 g/5 oz plain chocolate, broken into pieces

FILLING:

- 175 g/6 oz white chocolate, broken into pieces
- 4 tablespoons double cream
- 2 tablespoons brandy or rum

TO DECORATE:

- 50 g/2 oz plain chocolate, broken into pieces
- 25 g/1 oz white chocolate, broken into pieces
- small chocolate caraque or shavings (see pages 24–25) or edible gold leaf (optional)

1 Line a baking sheet with nonstick baking paper.

2 To make the chocolate cases, put the plain chocolate in a heatproof bowl over a saucepan of simmering water and leave until melted.

3 Spoon the melted chocolate into 24 paper sweet cases, spreading it up the sides with the back of a teaspoon. Invert the paper cases on to the prepared sheet and chill until set.

4 To make the filling, put the white chocolate into a heatproof bowl with the cream and leave over a saucepan of simmering water until melted. Stir in the brandy or rum. Leave until cool.

5 Spoon the liqueur cream into the chocolate cases until almost filled. Chill in the refrigerator until firm.

6 To decorate, melt the remaining plain and white chocolate in separate bowls. Spoon the white chocolate into a small piping bag fitted with a writing nozzle. (Alternatively, use a paper piping bag and snip off the merest tip.)

7 Spoon the plain chocolate over the filling in each case to seal it completely. Before the plain chocolate has set, pipe a circle of white chocolate on to it and draw a cocktail stick through it to give a feathered effect. Alternatively, pipe lattice lines.

8 If using the caraque and gold leaf to decorate, position them before the chocolate has set.

Makes 24

Raisin and Nut Clusters

Preparation time: 30 minutes, plus setting

- 250 g/8 oz raisins
- 250 g/8 oz hazelnuts, roasted and skinned
- 75 g/3 oz Almond Praline (see page 9), crushed
- 425 g/14 oz plain chocolate, melted
- 375 g/12 oz plain chocolate

1 Line two shallow trays or baking sheets with nonstick baking paper.

2 Combine the raisins, hazelnuts and crushed praline in a large bowl. Add the melted chocolate and stir the ingredients until thoroughly mixed.

3 To shape each cluster, take 1 teaspoonful of the mixture and, with the back of another teaspoon, push the cluster on to one of the paper-lined trays. Leave to set in a cool place for about *1 hour*.

4 Melt the plain chocolate in a heatproof bowl. With a fork or confectioner's dipping fork, dip the clusters into the chocolate. Allow excess chocolate to drip away and wipe the bottom of the fork on the bowl's edge. Let the clusters slide off the fork on to the paper on the second tray to harden. Put individual clusters in paper sweet cases to serve.

Makes 36

Chocolate Brazils

Preparation time: 20 minutes

- 175 g/6 oz plain chocolate
- 125 g/4 oz shelled Brazil nuts

1 Line a baking sheet with waxed or nonstick baking paper.

2 Break the chocolate into a heatproof bowl and set it over a pan of hot water to melt.

3 Using two forks, carefully dip each Brazil nut into the chocolate, coating it completely. Allow any surplus chocolate to drain against the side of the bowl before putting the nut on to the prepared baking sheet. The chocolate Brazils will keep for up to 4 weeks in an airtight tin.

Note: Not all the chocolate can be used for dipping as it becomes too shallow, and about 50 g/2 oz will be left in the bottom of the bowl. This can be used to make a few Raisin and Nut Clusters (see page 85).

Makes about 300 g/10 oz

variations _____

Chocolate Almonds

Use blanched almonds, coated singly in chocolate.

Chocolate Hazelnuts

Use skinned hazelnuts, coating them singly but arranging them in clusters of three to set.

Chocolate Date Squares

Preparation time: 20 minutes, plus cooling
Cooking time: 40 minutes
Oven temperature: 180°C (350°F), Gas Mark 4

- 250 g/8 oz chopped pitted
  dates
- 150 g/5 oz brown sugar
- 125 g/4 oz butter
- 125 ml/4 fl oz water
- 125 g/4 oz plain chocolate
- 2 eggs
- 175 g/6 oz self-raising flour

- 125 ml/4 fl oz orange juice
- 125 ml/4 fl oz milk
- 125 g/4 oz chopped walnuts
- walnut halves, to decorate

CHOCOLATE GLACE ICING:

- 200 g/7 oz icing sugar
- 1 tablespoon cocoa powder
- 1 teaspoon butter

1 Grease and flour a 30 x 25 cm/12 x 10 inch Swiss roll tin.

2 In a saucepan, combine the dates, sugar, butter and water. Heat until boiling, stirring to dissolve the sugar. Reduce the heat. Simmer, stirring, for *5 minutes* until the dates are soft.

3 Remove from the heat. Break the chocolate into pieces and stir in until melted. Set aside to cool.

4 Beat in the eggs 1 at a time. Sift the flour and stir into the chocolate mixture alternately with the orange juice and milk until the mixture is well blended. Fold in the chopped walnuts.

5 Spread the chocolate mixture evenly into the prepared tin and bake in a preheated oven, 180°C (350°F), Gas Mark 4, for about *30 minutes* until a cocktail stick inserted in the centre comes out clean. Allow to cool completely.

6 To make the icing, sift the icing sugar and cocoa powder into a small heatproof bowl. Melt the butter in 1 tablespoon of boiling water then add to the icing sugar, stirring well to make a smooth paste. Place the bowl over a saucepan of boiling water and stir for *1 minute*.

7 Pour the icing over the cake and smooth the surface with a spatula or a knife dipped in hot water. Cut the cake into squares and put a walnut half on the top of each one.

Makes about 30

Truffles

Preparation time: 20 minutes, plus cooling
Cooking time: 15–20 minutes

- 375 g/12 oz chocolate, broken into pieces
- 150 ml/¼ pint double cream
- 2–4 tablespoons brandy
- cocoa powder, for sifting
- Almond Praline (see page 9), crushed, or icing sugar, to decorate

1 Melt the chocolate in a heatproof bowl over a pan of simmering water, stirring occasionally until the chocolate is smooth. Remove the bowl from the heat.

2 Warm the cream in a small saucepan until tepid, and slowly pour it into the melted chocolate, stirring constantly. Leave the mixture to cool. Stir the brandy (according to taste) into the chocolate. Vigorously whisk the paste until it is lighter in colour and holds soft peaks. Chill until firm enough to shape by hand.

3 Sift a layer of cocoa powder on to a clean, dry work surface. Have the crushed praline or icing sugar ready to hand in a shallow bowl. Using a teaspoon, spoon out enough paste to form a 2.5 cm/1 inch ball. With another spoon, push the paste on to the cocoa powder. Shape each piece into a ball. Alternatively, roll and shape the balls in the crushed praline or icing sugar. Put the truffles in individual sweet paper cases for serving.

Makes 30

variation
Chocolate-coated Truffles

The truffles could also be coated in melted white chocolate. About 125 g/4 oz chocolate, melted, will coat about 16 truffles. Using a fork, dip the truffles, one at a time, in the melted chocolate, scraping the back of the fork on the side of the bowl as you lift it out, so that excess chocolate drips back into the bowl. Place the chocolate-coated truffles to set on a tray lined with nonstick baking paper. Leave in a cool place, but not in the refrigerator.

Fudge

Preparation time: 20 minutes, plus setting
Cooking time: 10–15 minutes

- 1 kg/2 lb granulated sugar
- 425 g/14 oz can sweetened
  condensed milk
- 125 g/4 oz butter
- 150 ml/¼ pint water

1 Oil a 25 x 15 cm/10 x 6 inch Swiss roll tin.

2 Place all the ingredients in a large saucepan. Stir over a medium heat until the sugar has dissolved and the butter has melted.

3 Bring to the boil and simmer, stirring continuously, until the fudge mixture reaches the soft ball stage. Test by putting a little of the mixture into a glass of iced water. It should form a soft ball.

4 Remove from the heat and beat vigorously until the mixture starts to thicken and turn granular. Pour into the prepared tin and cool until just set. Cut the fudge into squares, and store in an airtight container until required.

Makes 1.25 kg/2½ lb

variation
Chocolate Fudge

To make a chocolate version of the fudge, add 175 g/6 oz plain chocolate, broken into pieces, to the saucepan once removed from the heat, at step 4. Stir until melted, then proceed as for the main recipe.

Lemon Coconut Truffles

Preparation time: 30 minutes, plus cooling and freezing
Cooking time: 5 minutes

- 125 ml/4 fl oz double cream
- 250 g/8 oz white chocolate, chopped
- 3 teaspoons grated lemon rind
- 140 g/4½ oz desiccated coconut
- 8 drops lemon food colouring
- 3 teaspoons milk

1 Bring the cream slowly to the boil in a saucepan, stirring continuously. Remove the pan from the heat and stir in the chopped chocolate. Leave to stand for about *30 minutes* until cool.

2 Beat with an electric mixer until light and smooth. Blend in the lemon rind and 40 g/1½ oz coconut. Place teaspoons of the mixture on a foil-lined tray and freeze until hard.

3 Add the lemon colouring to the milk. Put the remaining coconut in a plastic bag, add the coloured milk and shake vigorously. Roll the truffle mixture into balls and roll them in coloured coconut. Keep refrigerated until ready to serve.

Makes about 30

Orange Turkish Delight

Preparation time: 20 minutes, plus setting
Cooking time: 20 minutes

- 300 ml/½ pint water
- grated rind of 2 oranges
- grated rind of 1 lemon
- 40 g/1½ oz gelatine
- 500 g/1 lb sugar
- 4 tablespoons orange juice
- 2 tablespoons orange flower water
- 250 g/8 oz icing sugar, sifted
- 2 tablespoons cornflour

1 Place 150 ml/¼ pint of the water and the orange and lemon rinds in a pan. Bring to the boil and simmer for *10 minutes*.

2 In a separate pan, boil the remaining water and pour into a small basin. Sprinkle over the gelatine and stir until dissolved.

3 Lower the heat under the first pan and add the sugar, dissolved gelatine, orange juice and orange flower water. Stir with a metal spoon until the sugar has dissolved. Bring to the boil and continue boiling for *10 minutes*.

4 Strain into a wetted 18 cm/7 inch square tin. Allow to cool and leave overnight to set.

5 Mix together the icing sugar and cornflour and sprinkle a thin layer on to a work surface.

6 With a wet knife, loosen the edges of the Turkish delight. Dip the base of the tin into hot water for *4 seconds* and turn the delight out on to the icing sugar and cornflour mixture.

7 Cut into 36 pieces, place in a large polythene bag with the remaining sugar mixture and shake gently to coat the pieces thoroughly.

8 Place in wooden boxes, or tins, between sheets of non-stick baking paper, sprinkling any sugar mixture left in the polythene bag over each layer.

9 The orange turkish delight will keep for up to 2 weeks.

Makes about 36

Fudge-topped Gingerbread

Preparation time: 40 minutes
Cooking time: 1½ hours
Oven temperature: 150°C (300°F), Gas Mark 2

- **175 g/6 oz brown sugar**
- **125 g/4 oz margarine, softened**
- **200 g/7 oz golden syrup**
- **50 g/2 oz black treacle**
- **425 g/14 oz plain flour**
- **1½ teaspoons baking powder**
- **½ teaspoon bicarbonate of soda**
- **2 teaspoons ground ginger**
- **1 egg**
- **150 ml/¼ pint milk**
- **125 g/4 oz chopped walnuts**

FUDGE ICING:
- **250 g/8 oz icing sugar, sifted**
- **50 g/2 oz margarine, softened**
- **3 tablespoons milk**

1 Grease and line a 23 cm/9 inch square cake tin.

2 Place the sugar, margarine, golden syrup and treacle in a saucepan. Heat gently, stirring constantly, until the sugar has dissolved. Leave to cool.

3 Sift together the flour, baking powder, bicarbonate of soda and ground ginger.

4 Pour over the cooled syrup and add the egg and milk. Beat until smooth.

5 Pour the mixture into the prepared tin. Bake in a preheated oven, 150°C (300°F), Gas Mark 2, for *1½ hours*. Leave in the tin, set on a wire rack, to cool.

6 To make the fudge icing, place the icing sugar, margarine and milk in a heatproof bowl over a pan of hot water and stir until the icing is smooth and glossy.

7 Remove from the heat and allow to cool. When cold, beat until the icing has thickened.

8 Swirl the icing over the top of the cooled gingerbread and sprinkle with the chopped walnuts. Leave to set, then cut into 16 squares.

9 Pack the gingerbread in a tin or box or wrap individual pieces in cellophane. It can be stored for up to 2 weeks in an airtight container.

Makes 16 squares

Almonds 72-3
  almond praline 7
  chocolate almonds 86
  fresh strawberry and almond
    tartlets 64
  nougat 82
  raisin and nut clusters 85
  tarte aux pommes à la Normande
    52
  Twelfth Night frangipane
    cake 56
amaretti biscuits: raspberry and
  amaretti tartlets 64
apples: apple strip tart 54
  blackberry and apple crumble 48
  moist apple-spice cake 78
  tarte aux pommes à la Normande
    52
  toffee apple pudding 47
apricot tart 54

Baking blind 9
bananas: banana cake 71
  banana rum fritters 43
  bananas with chocolate fudge
    sauce 31
biscuits: ginger shortbread 69
  gingerbread men 69
blackberry and apple crumble 48
blackcurrant tart 60
blueberries: raspberry and
  blueberry tart 60
Brazils, chocolate 86
brownies, double chocolate 30

Cakes: banana cake 71
  chocolate fudge cake 32
  coffee and walnut layer cake 76
  Devil's food cake 22
  double chocolate brownies 30
  Florentine slices 70
  fudge-topped gingerbread 94
  lemon cream sponge 77
  moist apple-spice cake 78
  no-cook chocolate nut slice 68
  passion cake 74
  strawberry cake 79
  Twelfth Night frangipane
    cake 56
  white and dark truffle cake 16
caramel: almond praline 7
caraque, chocolate 24
carrots: passion cake 74
cheese, soft: fresh strawberry and
  almond tartlets 64
  tiramisu 41
cheesecake, classic French 44
chocolate 7, 10-35
  bananas with chocolate fudge
    sauce 31
  chocolate almonds 86
  chocolate Brazils 86
  chocolate-coated truffles 89
  chocolate date squares 88
  chocolate éclairs 63

chocolate fondue 27
chocolate fudge 90
chocolate fudge cake 32
chocolate hazelnuts 86
chocolate liqueur crêpes 15
chocolate liqueur cups 84
chocolate meringue stacks 12
chocolate mousse 26
chocolate roulade 20
decadent chocolate tart 34
decorations 24-5
Devil's food cake 22
double chocolate brownies 30
double chocolate chip ice
  cream 18
Florentine slices 70
mocha sauce 28
mud pies 35
no-cook chocolate nut slice 68
pears à la Belle Hélène 14
profiteroles 19
raisin and nut clusters 85
steamed chocolate sponge 28
truffles 89
white and dark truffle cake 16
choux pastry: chocolate éclairs 63
  profiteroles 19
coconut: Florentine slices 70
  lemon coconut truffles 92
coffee: coffee and walnut layer
    cake 76
  Devil's food cake 22
  mocha sauce 28
  tiramisu 41
  white and dark truffle cake 16
cream: mango fool 40
  rhubarb fool 38
crème patissière 8
crêpes, chocolate liqueur 15
crumbles: blackberry and apple
    crumble 48
  rhubarb and orange crumble 48

Dates: chocolate date squares 88
decadent chocolate tart 34
decorations 72-3
  chocolate 24-5
Devil's food cake 22
double chocolate brownies 30
double chocolate chip ice
  cream 18
dried fruit: Florentine slices 70

Eclairs, chocolate 63
equipment 6-7

Florentine slices 70
flowers, frosted 72
fondue, chocolate 27
fools: mango fool 40
  rhubarb fool 38
frangipane cake, Twelfth Night 56
French cheesecake 44
fritters, banana rum 43
frosted decorations 72

fruit 7
  chocolate fondue 27
fudge 90
  bananas with chocolate fudge
    sauce 31
  chocolate fudge 90
fudge cake, chocolate 32
fudge-topped gingerbread 94

Gifts 80-94
ginger: fudge-topped ginger-
    bread 94
  ginger shortbread 69
  gingerbread men 69
glacé cherries: nougat 82
Grand Marnier: chocolate liqueur
    crêpes 15

Hazelnuts 73
  chocolate hazelnuts 86
  plum tart 62
  raisin and nut clusters 85

Ice cream, double chocolate
    chip 18

Leaves: chocolate 25
  frosted 72
lemon: lemon coconut truffles 92
  lemon cream sponge 77
lime meringue pie 42
liqueurs: chocolate liqueur
    crêpes 15
  chocolate liqueur cups 84

Mango fool 40
mascarpone cheese: tiramisu 41
meringues: chocolate meringue
    stacks 12
  lime meringue pie 42
mocha sauce 28
moist apple-spice cake 78
mousse, chocolate 26
mud pies 35

No-cook chocolate nut slice 68
nougat 82
nuts: chocolate-dipped nuts 24
  no-cook chocolate nut slice 68
  see also almonds, walnuts etc

Orange: chocolate liqueur
    crêpes 15
  orange Turkish delight 93
  passionfruit curd tart 57
  rhubarb and orange crumble 48

Passion cake 74
passionfruit curd tart 57
pastry: baking blind 9
  pâte brisée 8-9
  pâte sucrée 8
  rolling out 9
pâte brisée 8-9
pâte sucrée 8

pâtisserie 50-64
pears: pears à la Belle Hélène 14
  tarte aux poires 58
pecan nuts 73
physalis, chocolate-dipped 25
pie, lime meringue 42
plum tart 62
praline, almond 7
profiteroles 19

Raisin and nut clusters 85
raspberry and amaretti tartlets 64
rhubarb: rhubarb and orange
    crumble 48
  rhubarb fool 38
  rhubarb tart 53
rose leaves, chocolate 25
roulade, chocolate 20
raspberry and blueberry tart 60
rum: banana rum fritters, 43

Sauce, mocha 28
shortbread, ginger 69
sponge cake: lemon cream
    sponge 77
steamed puddings: steamed
    chocolate sponge 28
  treacle sponge 46
strawberries: chocolate-dipped
    strawberries 25
  fresh strawberry and almond
    tartlets 64
  strawberry cake 79
sweets: chocolate almonds 86
  chocolate Brazils 86
  chocolate-coated truffles 89
  chocolate date squares 88
  chocolate fudge 90
  chocolate hazelnuts 86
  chocolate liqueur cups 84
  fudge 90
  lemon coconut truffles 92
  nougat 82
  orange Turkish delight 93
  raisin and nut clusters 85
  truffles 89

Tarts: apple strip tart 54
  apricot tart 54
  blackcurrant tart 60
  decadent chocolate tart 34
  fresh strawberry and almond
    tartlets 64
  lime meringue pie 42
  mud pies 35
  passionfruit curd tart 57
  plum tart 62
  raspberry and amaretti tartlets 64
  raspberry and blueberry tart 60
  rhubarb tart 53
  tarte aux poires 58
  tarte aux pommes à la Normande
    52
tiramisu 41
toffee apple pudding 47

treacle sponge 46
truffles 89
  chocolate-coated truffles 89
  lemon coconut truffles 92
Turkish delight, orange 93
Twelfth Night frangipane cake 56

Walnuts 73
  chocolate date squares 88
  coffee and walnut layer cake 76
  double chocolate brownies 30
  fudge-topped gingerbread 94
white and dark truffle cake 16

Special Photography:
Philip Webb
Jacket Photography:
Sean Myers
Other Photography:
Reed Consumer Books
Ltd./Howard Allman /Bryce
Attwell /Steve Baxter /Theo
Bergstrom /Martin Brigdale /Laurie
Evans /Paul Grater /Christine
Hanscomb /Paul Kerry /Graham
Kirk /Vernon Morgan /Roger
Stowell /Philip Webb /Paul
Williams
Special Photography Home
Economist:
Sarah Ramsbottom
Jacket Home Economist:
Sunil Vijayakar